Obsidian Orchids

Obsidian Orchids

Faithfulness in the Building of Zion

ATTILA TAKACS

RESOURCE *Publications* · Eugene, Oregon

OBSIDIAN ORCHIDS
Faithfulness in the Building of Zion

Resource Publications
An Imprint of Wipf and Stock Publishers
199 W. 8th Ave., Suite 3
Eugene, OR 97401

www.wipfandstock.com

PAPERBACK ISBN: 979-8-3852-8065-0
HARDCOVER ISBN: 979-8-3852-8066-7
EBOOK ISBN: 979-8-3852-8067-4

VERSION NUMBER 05/21/26

For those who learned
that holiness is not noise
but endurance.

For those who chose
to carry water
instead of wood.

May the Unseen Father
steady your hands.

Contents

Author's Note

I AM A HUNGARIAN Ashkenazi Christian Jew, based in Scotland. Part of my inheritance carries Jewish covenant memory—names, losses, blessings, and the stubborn insistence that the past is not decoration but responsibility. Another part carries a long Hungarian Christian memory—devotion so old it can feel like weather.

The irony is not lost on me: I grew up Catholic, was wounded there as a child, and still could not discard what was holy. Some things stayed in my hands like bread. Not because the Church is flawless, but because Jesus Christ remains faithful to His people across her histories, even when His people falter. I write as one who trusts the historic confession of Father, Son, and Holy Spirit. Any renewal worth having will be a return to Christ, not a new throne.

This is my second theological book with Wipf and Stock. My first, *Pale Bloom* (December 2025), was written from the place where grace interrupts wounds and refuses to leave. *Obsidian Orchids* is written from a steadier place: the long work of covenant—how mercy becomes public, how holiness becomes ordinary, how Zion is built by walkers rather than performers.

I do not claim the authority of prophet or ruler, and I do not seek disciples. I offer testimony and formation, not a new system. If anything in these pages feels excessive, weigh it by Scripture, by the Church's long memory, and by the steady counsel of the trustworthy.

When I speak of "mysticism," I do not mean secret powers or rival revelation. I mean leaning so deeply into prayer and discipleship that Jesus Christ becomes the most solid reality—and the fruit returns as mercy at the table, in the hallway, in the confessional, in the everyday places where love costs something.

Mysticism is not spectacle. It is a life that becomes kinder under pressure.

INTRODUCTION

A Faith That Refuses to Forget

THIS BOOK IS FOR readers who love God but have learned—often quietly—that the story they were handed feels incomplete. Not false. Incomplete. As if certain rooms in the house of faith stayed locked, not because they were wicked, but because they were inconvenient.

These pages are a field guide for living covenant life in public: building Zion through ordinary acts that make room for the vulnerable, tell the truth without cruelty, and let mercy become shared life.

Zion, as I use the word, is not a slogan or a fantasy city. It is what faith looks like when it grows hands. If "Zion" isn't your native vocabulary, hear it as the same holy hunger: the kingdom of God made visible—the city of God glimpsed in kitchens, budgets, parish halls, Relief Society rooms, and the hard work of becoming a people.

WHERE I AM WRITING FROM

My roots are Catholic and Evangelical. I was formed by a sacramental imagination—grace meeting us in ordinary matter—and by a fierce love for Scripture, repentance, and personal faith that refuses performance.

I trust the creeds and the historic confession of Father, Son, and Holy Spirit. I also trust that the Spirit has never stopped calling Christians to reform, repair, and return—again and again—to the mercy of Jesus Christ.

If you feel protective of your tradition, you're not alone. I'm not asking you to abandon it. I'm inviting you into deeper fidelity within it.

You'll also notice a seriousness about Zion, covenant, and communal responsibility. When I use Restorationist language, I'm speaking as someone shaped by the wider Latter-day Saint movement, but not primarily by a Utah/Salt Lake City–centered institutional frame. My instincts were formed more by the reforming, Christ-centered, peaceable stream associated with Joseph Smith III and the earlier RLDS (now Community of Christ) tradition: Zion as a lived ethic—accountable, communal, resistant to triumphalism.

As of this writing, I am not formally Community of Christ. I don't claim that identity or speak for that communion. What I carry forward is not a party label, but a discipline: Zion as something you do to your life together, not something you merely claim about your beliefs.

I also come to these questions as a Hungarian Ashkenazi Jew, with real respect for both Latter-day Saints and Community of Christ. I recognize in them a seriousness about covenant, community, and belonging, even if I do not find myself fully at home within their frameworks.

For much of my life I have been a walker between traditions—a friendly face at many tables, unwilling to belong cheaply or force my faith beneath a banner too soon.

So I remain a disciple still in motion—but no longer without direction.

WHAT THIS BOOK WILL FEEL LIKE

This book is not written to be admired. It is written to be used.

Each lesson follows the same rhythm: reflection, story, and concrete practice—because covenant is not only something you believe. It is bread and speech and money and rest. It is the daily decision to make room for someone—or to quietly push them out.

You will move through kitchens and classrooms, burdens carried in silence, Sabbath as breath, the ethics of wealth and power, and the small ways a community becomes either Zion or something harsher.

Think of these lessons as maps: not perfect diagrams, but true orientations—enough to help you walk with fewer false routes and fewer performed versions of holiness.

If you are tired of religion as theater, this book is for you. If you want depth without the demand to pretend, this book is for you. If you have been wounded by religion—trained to fear honest questions, taught to confuse exhaustion with holiness—this book is for you too.

Read slowly. Take breaks. Let these pages become a place to breathe, not another place to prove yourself.

And one more thing: the "you" in these pages is not a courtroom voice hunting for a defendant. It is an invitation—sometimes gentle, sometimes urgent—because love does not always whisper. If a sentence lands close to the bone, hear it as a call to honesty, not a verdict.

SCRIPTURE, TRADITION, AND THE WORLD BEHIND THE BIBLE

Many modern Christians read the Bible as if it descended from heaven fully formed, sealed, and self-interpreting. In reality, Scripture emerged from a living religious ecosystem—and for many Christians (including Catholics), it has always been read inside a living memory: worship, prayer, teaching, and the steady rule of faith that keeps interpretation anchored to Jesus Christ.

Jesus and the first Jewish followers of the Way inhabited a world saturated with covenant memory, empire pressure, hope for God's reign, and a thick awareness that reality has layers—seen and unseen. To recover that atmosphere is not to add a new gospel. It is to hear the old one with clean ears.

If names like *1 Enoch* and *Jubilees* are unfamiliar, think of them as nearby voices from the Jewish world surrounding the Bible—texts many believers read in the centuries just before and around the time of Jesus. They are not treated here as "new Scripture," and they do not replace the canon. Scripture remains the compass.

These writings function as a chorus that helps certain themes sound in their original air: the moral seriousness of history, the weight of judgment, the hope of restoration, and the way evil can behave like a regime. Everything in this book is read toward Jesus Christ, not away from him.

WHAT IS 1 ENOCH?

First Enoch is an ancient collection of writings attributed to Enoch (the figure in Genesis who "walked with God"). It imagines a world where heaven and earth are not sealed off: angels, rebellion, corruption, judgment, and the promise that God will set things right.

It is vivid, symbolic, sometimes strange—but it helps modern readers recover something the New Testament often assumes: spiritual evil is not only "personal temptation." It can become organized, entrenched, oppressive—almost like a system.

Zion matters here because Zion isn't private goodness. It is God's peace pressing into public life.

Bottom line: Evil loves anonymity; covenant names it.

WHAT IS JUBILEES?

Jubilees is an ancient retelling of Genesis and early Exodus. It reshapes the story to highlight covenant identity, holiness, Sabbath patterns, and the idea that time itself can be redeemed.

It is especially concerned with what it looks like for a people to live as God's community in the real world—how they order their lives, remember their story, resist assimilation, and practice faithfulness across generations.

It presses a simple question: *What does covenant look like when it becomes a culture?*

WHERE DOES THE BOOK OF MORMON FIT IN?

The Book of Mormon belongs to a different category—not an ancient Jewish companion text, but a modern Restoration witness brought forth through Joseph Smith. For Latter-day Saints, it stands as another testament of Jesus Christ and a foundational scripture that calls a people into covenant, repentance, and gathering.

For Catholic and other non-Restoration readers, you may not relate to it as scripture in the same way. This book will not ask you to pretend otherwise.

Here is how I will use it: as a Restoration witness to Christ and to Zion themes—not as a rival canon, not as an ecclesial test, not as something imposed upon anyone's conscience.

I will ask something simpler: notice how communities are formed by the texts they pray with, argue over, and try—however imperfectly—to live. In that sense the Book of Mormon matters here because it repeatedly shows how societies rise and fall through pride, inequality, violence, and care (or neglect) for the poor.

In the Joseph Smith III stream that formed me, it was often approached less as a weapon for winning arguments and more as a moral and spiritual tutor: a Christ-centered witness meant to form a people. Its deepest value is not merely in being proved, but in being lived—drawing readers toward Jesus, repentance, peacemaking, covenant responsibility, and the practical ethics of Zion.

Put simply: 1 Enoch and Jubilees help us hear the Bible's world more clearly. The Book of Mormon carries that same Zion-hunger into modern faith as it is lived within Restoration traditions. Read with humility, these texts don't replace the Bible—they help us ask better questions about what Zion meant then and what Zion requires now.

Bottom line: Zion is the gospel made habitable.

NAMING GOD: LANGUAGE, REVERENCE, AND MEMORY

You will notice names and phrases that may feel unfamiliar at first. God is sometimes referred to as *Adonai* ("Lord"), a Jewish title of reverence. The Holy Spirit is sometimes named *Ruach*—breath, wind—the life-giving presence of God.

These aren't meant to sound exotic. They are reminders: faith did not begin in English, and the words we choose shape the way we imagine God.

You will also encounter the phrase *Unseen Father*. This is not a new doctrine and not a replacement for Scripture or the creeds. It is memory-language—the way I learned to address the Father in prayer with reverence and carefulness.

The phrase comes from a time when it felt like everyone had left me behind, and yet God began to show up—not as a figure I could point to, but as Presence: as if love and sorrow could take form.

I will keep the story brief. Beneath my often-rigid childhood Catholic world, something unhealthy was also growing in the shadows: a neo-gnostic strain of spirituality—"secret knowledge" talk that promised light but produced confusion, control, and fear. I was pulled into it as a child through family tragedy and a grandmother who, for reasons I still grieve, had lost much of her tenderness long before I was old enough to protect myself.

In my first book, *Pale Bloom*, I spoke of that experience only as much as necessary—for wounded men and women who needed mending, not more darkness. This book, *Obsidian Orchids*, has a different aim. It is focused on Zion-building—on covenant life, communal responsibility, and learning to stay awake to how darkness works. So here I speak of those early shadows only in outline, because this is more defense than excavation.

I am not inviting you into "gnosis." I am warning against it: the rot that hollows out Christianity by turning faith into private secrets, spiritual elitism, and distrust of ordinary goodness.

Whatever language I use, my intent is the same: to keep mystery holy, not to redraw the faith. I hold to the heart of Christian confession:

God the Father is real.
Christ is the true Light.
And the Spirit is God's living breath among us.

An Image That Steadied Me

I do not offer this as doctrine or prediction, only as a personal vision that steadied me while writing—an image of what it means to remain faithful without feeding the fire.

UNTIL THEY REMEMBER

I once saw our house burning.

It did not collapse.

It burned the way homes burn when they have been inhabited too long by fear. The roof still held. The walls still stood. But the windows breathed smoke, and the doors were hot to the touch.

My brothers and sisters were gathered outside.

Some stood close to the walls, shouting. They argued about who struck the match, whose fault it was, which room mattered most, which wall should be saved first. They named each other enemies and called it righteousness. Their words were dry wood.

Others were already walking away. They carried what they could bear. Some were angry. Some were grieving. Some could not stop looking back. They said peace required distance. They said the house was already lost.

I stood between them, unseen.

The shouting ones were blind with heat.
The departing ones were blind with sorrow.

I wanted to leave too. I was tired of shouting and afraid of burning. But something held me still—a weight in my chest that felt like grief, or maybe love.

Then I understood.

The house was not empty.

I crossed the threshold.

The heat stole my breath. The floor was blackened but firm. Smoke moved along the ceiling like a living thing.

And in the center of the house, our Father stood.

He was not frantic.
He was not defeated.

He moved with the steadiness of One who knows the weight of fire. He drew water from a well that did not run dry and cast it where the flames were strongest. Some places cooled. Others flared when left unattended.

He looked at me, and the fire did not stop.

"Father," I said. "They are fighting outside. Others are leaving. I am afraid of both."

"I know," He answered.

"I do not want to leave You alone in this house."

He regarded me—not with surprise, not with flattery, but with truth. There were marks in His hands that the fire did not erase.

"As long as I remain," He said, "the house stands."

I wept—not from smoke, but from the weight of it.

"What if no one comes back?" I asked. "What if they only shout or flee?"

He lifted the water again.

"Not all who are Mine will run," He said. "And not all who run are lost."

Then He placed a dark orchid in my hands—its petals like cooled stone, its heart alive and unburned.

"This grew where the fire passed and did not consume," He said. "Carry it."

"What should I do?"

"Go," He said. "Do not add to the shouting. Do not bless the leaving. Tend the fire where you stand. Forgive when you are pressed to bite. Love your brothers and sisters even when they forget they are family."

"And You?"

"I remain," He said, and His voice did not strain. "Until they remember where their home is. Until they remember who I am."

The flames roared behind Him.
The well did not run dry.

I stepped back into the night, the orchid steady in my palm.

Outside, nothing had been resolved. The arguments continued. The departures continued. The night was loud with fear and certainty and grief.

But the fire no longer felt like a verdict.

It felt like a passage.

The Unseen Father was still inside.

Not pacing.
Not negotiating.
Remaining.

Where the water fell, the flames learned their limits.

The orchid did not glow. It did not demand attention. It simply lived—rooted in scorched ground, unashamed of surviving heat without becoming ash.

I understood what it meant to remain without feeding the fire.

Not to deny the burning.
Not to sanctify it.
Not to flee it.

But to walk back into the night carrying what the flames could not claim.

The house still stands.

The Father still remains.

And until they remember—

there will be those sent into the smoke, not as arsonists or deserters, but as witnesses:

bearing water,
bearing life,
bearing what the fire passed through
and could not consume.

LESSON ONE

Cartography of the Quiet Compass

THE HOLY SPIRIT DOES not merely steer you toward a better life. He forms a holy posture within you—in communion with Jesus Christ, confessed with the Church across her histories—until mercy becomes shared life instead of a private mood.

We keep mistaking guidance for relocation, self-improvement, or private intuition. But the Spirit is Presence: He converts the heart, then binds that converted heart into communion.

You love maps—the paper kind and the private ones you carry in your chest: rules for tenderness, rules for guarding, rules for what counts as "real life," and what still feels like a waiting room.

Maps can be gifts. They keep you from getting lost.

But maps can also become armor. Ink becomes permission to remain unseen. Borders harden into identity because it feels safer than letting the Unseen Father name you Himself—the Father we confess in the Name of Father, Son, and Holy Spirit. A circled city becomes destiny: *Once I get there, I will be whole.* A shaded neighborhood becomes a curse: *Nothing good can come from here.*

Sometimes we do not use maps to find our way. We use them to avoid being known.

Grace begins here: Jesus Christ does not wait for bravery before He comes near. He took flesh, walked ordinary roads, entered the rooms we keep locked, and did not flinch at the Cross. Mercy is not a theory. Mercy became a body.

Adonai has always spoken—sometimes with fire and thunder, more often with tenderness. Elijah names the pattern: "And after the fire a sound of sheer silence" (1 Kgs 19:12).

This is how the Ruach ha-Kodesh moves: quiet, steady, patient. Not forcing entry. Waiting to be welcomed.

You can rearrange geography a thousand times while the same prison travels with you. But the Unseen Father does not merely visit. He indwells. Paul treats this as fact: "Do you not know that you are God's temple and that God's Spirit dwells in you?" (1 Cor 3:16).

So the compass is not a personality trait.
It is a Presence.

I receive this Restoration witness[1] with gratitude: "If ye will enter in by the way, and receive the Holy Ghost, it will show unto you all things what ye should do" (2 Nephi 32:5). The Spirit guides. The heart consents.

And for Christians formed in sacramental traditions, consent is not meant to stay private. The Ruach is given in Christ's Body: water pressed to the forehead and a name spoken; a Host placed into open hands; a line of the penitent; the priest's quiet "I absolve you"; the Church's long obedience—wounded, still beloved. The Spirit does not manufacture solitary mystics. He forms communion.

Jewish-rooted witnesses echo the same moral and covenantal truth Scripture already insists upon. Enoch warns with clarity: "Love uprightness and walk therein. . . . Walk in righteousness, my sons, and it shall guide you on good paths" (1 Enoch 91:4–5). Wisdom refuses to become a tool for the barricaded heart.

The order keeps repeating through the covenant story: Adonai gives Himself first. Covenant is not only command. It is mercy that reshapes the interior. Jubilees names the surgery: "I will circumcise the foreskin of their heart . . . and I will create in them a holy spirit" (Jubilees 1:22).

1. I use "Restoration witness" in reference to voices shaped by the Book of Mormon tradition.

This is the quiet compass: the Ruach forming a people from the inside out until holiness stops being atmosphere and becomes communal ethic—hands and speech and bread and forgiveness.

Zion is not an idea.
Zion is mercy with an address.

MIRIAM AND THE MAP THAT ATE HER

Let this land in ordinary life.

There was a girl once. We will call her Miriam, because the name carries history.

She was born in a small border town: a factory, a river that sometimes shone, a few streets nobody bragged about. In late summer the air smelled faintly of metal and cut grass. As a child she loved it. She knew the fig tree. She believed the rusted tracks were silver roads.

Then she grew, and the world arrived in blue light and casual contempt. Screens taught her what "counted." Voices from elsewhere laughed at towns like hers: dead end, stagnant, nowhere. They praised cities with stations and cafés, and treated movement as virtue—as if leaving proved you were chosen.

Miriam felt the sting and did not know what to do with it. Part of her wanted to defend home. Another part feared being laughed at. So she swallowed their disdain like medicine. At first she hid it. Then it became fluent. She learned the currency of distance: irony, the practiced shrug, the sneer that sounds like sophistication.

At a dinner, someone asked where she was from. A small pause caught in her throat—the moment where truth costs something.

So she performed. "Just a small place. Nothing there."

They laughed—warm laughter, approval. Miriam felt relief, and then felt the relief rot into shame. She learned a lesson she would spend years unlearning: contempt can be rewarded.

That reward had consequences. It trained her tongue to betray her beginnings. It made her feel safer in rooms that were not hers, and colder toward the people who had loved her before she was impressive. The map did not simply guide her out. It taught her to despise what had formed her.

Contempt is a cheap passport. It gets you into rooms and locks you out of yourself.

Miriam's sickness is not rare. Whole families inherit it. People learn to buy belonging by selling pieces of themselves.

But Adonai did not teach Abraham that holiness is a relocation package. He taught him a posture that survives deserts and apartments alike: "I am God Almighty; walk before me, and be blameless" (Gen 17:1). Allegiance, not address. *Walk before me.*

And because Jesus Christ has already walked toward us—even into our contempt and self-protection—we are free to practice a different posture. The Shepherd calls by name, not by postcode. When you let Him name you, the compass corrects not only where your feet go, but what your heart worships.

THE INVERSION THAT EXPOSES US

Miriam's map is one version of the disease. There is another.

Some swallow shame until it drowns them. Others drink the opposite poison: they inflate their soil into entitlement and wield nationalism like a sacrament. Both diseases share the same delusion: distance determines worth.

Places matter. Land remembers. Mercy passes through a place and leaves it gentler; violence passes through and leaves it flinching. And yet salvation is not stored in soil.

Adonai steadies territorial arrogance with one sentence: "The land shall not be sold in perpetuity, for the land is mine; with me you are but aliens and tenants" (Lev 25:23). *Mine,* He says. And if the land is His, so are you.

So ask the truer question: not *Where is the holy land?* but *Where is the holy posture?*

And deeper still: *Who is already standing with me here?*

THE KINGDOM YOU CANNOT RELOCATE INTO

Jesus Christ speaks with a simplicity that still offends cleverness: "The kingdom of God is among you" (Luke 17:21). Not a souvenir. A reign. Not a distant project. A present Shepherd.

The kingdom begins in the heart and becomes visible in the hands: forgiveness, truth told when lying would protect your image, mercy practiced when no one is watching. Places matter, but no one relocates into Zion.

Zion is built within because grace takes root within, and then it spills outward: a people learning covenant fidelity together, learning to carry one another's burdens. In the Restoration family—and in peace-and-justice–shaped streams like Community of Christ—Zion is named in precisely this key: covenant embodied as communal responsibility, not institutional conquest. And in the catholic fullness of the Christian tradition, that same embodied mercy is given sacramental grammar: one bread, one cup, one body learning to become what it receives.

We are not building Zion alone. Jesus Christ builds with us. The Cross is where mercy became flesh. The Resurrection is the promise that mercy is not fragile. And the Church—bruised and radiant with saints—is where that mercy is meant to take a shared shape.

The Spirit's guidance is not a private badge. It is shared belonging. Christ converts the heart, then teaches that converted heart how to live as communion.

PRACTICE

Not big gestures. Small obediences with real weight.

1. **Name the place you secretly despise.** Write its name on paper. Then write one concrete sentence of gratitude (a person, a meal, a protection, a mercy). Read it aloud once.
2. **Before one major decision this week, set a ninety-second timer.** Ask: *Is this obedience, or avoidance?* Don't negotiate. When the timer ends, write one line: "I am choosing ___

because ___." (If you know the Ignatian Examen, use it: What draws you toward communion, and what makes you curl inward?)

3. **Do one hidden act of mercy where you actually live.** Choose something embodied and verifiable: clean one neglected corner, repair one small thing, speak dignity to one person you usually rush past. Offer it as worship—a small Eucharistic echo in daily matter.

Home is not found by distance.
Home is found by turning—again, and again.

Let the map fall away.
Keep the quiet compass.

LESSON TWO

Cartography of the Unseen Burden

Every year it returns. Late summer thins into autumn, and the sayings drift back in like smoke you did not invite:

Teaching is a waste.
Kids will drain you dry.
If you work with the young, you must not have made it elsewhere.

Many of us swallowed that contempt because we were trained on the wrong scale. Anything slow, repetitive, or unseen gets filed under consolation, not calling.

Jesus Christ refuses that scale.

He took children—interrupting and needy—and placed them at the center: "Let the little children come to me, and do not stop them; for it is to such as these that the kingdom of God belongs" (Luke 18:16).

And in the Restoration witness that shaped my early spiritual imagination, the scene is even more intimate: "He took their little children, one by one, and blessed them, and prayed unto the Father for them" (3 Nephi 17:21).

The kingdom is not earned by importance. It is received open-handed. Christ opened His arms to us; we are free to open ours to them.

HADASSAH AND THE ROOM THAT SMELLS LIKE DUST AND MILK

There is a woman, Hadassah.

Each morning she steps into a room that smells of dust, crayons, and spilled milk. Yesterday's half-erased sentences cling to the board. A chair scrapes. A marker cap is missing. Her coffee cools again.

Then the children arrive, not as a neat class but as fragments.

One laughs too loudly, using jokes as armor. One comes silent, scanning corners for danger. One clutches a book like a lifeline. One has not eaten properly in two days and hides hunger behind attitude.

Hadassah knows their names and their storms. Some mornings she feels the pressure in her chest: I am not enough for this.

In the corridor, adults mutter the old contempt: "It'll drain you." "If you ended up teaching, you didn't make it higher." They see tiredness and assume the work is small.

They do not see what Adonai sees.

Hadassah does not need a podium. She needs patience that survives a bell schedule, mercy that returns after misunderstanding, steadiness that keeps coming back. Under the noise she returns to a quieter truth that is not self-talk but grace:

This is not punishment.
This is trust.

Holiness rarely looks impressive. It often wears a lanyard.

THE WEIGHT AND THE STAKES

To guide a child is not a curse. It is a holy burden.

It is heavy because lives can be crushed by neglect, cruelty, indifference, and the slow poison of being unseen. The weight is not proof the work is low. It is proof the stakes are real.

And Jesus Christ does not assign holy burdens and then watch from a distance. The Cross is God entering what drains us—without contempt, without retreat.

Neglect is not neutral. Forgetting is a quiet disaster.

"A generation . . . who did not know the LORD or the work that he had done for Israel" (Judg 2:10). No plague. No fireworks. Only drift.

So Adonai commands what looks ordinary but is survival: "Recite them to your children" (Deut 6:7). Formation is always happening; the only question is what—or Who—is doing the forming.

Across her histories, the Church has been blunt about this. Children are not interruptions. They are persons entrusted to us. The world's contempt is not "realism." It is a polite kind of violence that trains the young to believe they are disposable.

FORMATION, NOT POSSESSION

The young do not merely need information. They need formation: a room where light can be recognized.

Yet no teacher can manufacture a new heart. That boundary is mercy. It keeps love from becoming control.

Hadassah has learned it the hard way. Her task is to cultivate, warn, bless, and correct—to build a room where truth is speakable, mercy is practiced, and repair is possible.

The Unseen Father takes responsibility for the deeper miracle: "A new heart I will give you . . . and a new spirit I will put within you" (Ezek 36:26). "They look on the outward appearance, but the LORD looks on the heart" (1 Sam 16:7).

Ecclesial humility matters here. No one "saves" a child by force of personality. Salvation belongs to Christ. Teachers participate; they do not replace. The Ruach forms by communion—through patience, discipline, and the slow insistence that a child is worth the trouble.

HADASSAH, THE LAMP, AND THE BOY WITH BALLED FISTS

Watch her with the boy in the third row.

His fists stay balled as if ready for war. He mocks tenderness. He strikes first so he will not be struck. When he laughs, it is not joy. It is warning.

Hadassah feels the instinct to protect herself by hardening. If she hardens, she will win the moment and lose the child.

So she chooses a different risk. She gives him a problem she knows he can solve if he slows down. She offers competence instead of shame, and then she waits.

Silence presses. His jaw tightens. For a moment it looks like he might flip the desk and prove everyone right. Then something in him leans forward. The answer arrives, small and stubborn, like a candle catching.

Hadassah nods once. "You see more than you pretend."

In him, something loosens—just a notch. A thought he does not know how to say forms anyway: I am capable of more than destruction.

Ancient Jewish witness literature names this kind of mercy breaking in: "And light shall appear unto them" (1 Enoch 1:8). I hear Enoch and Jubilees as Jewish-rooted echoes—lanterns that help us recognize what the prophets and apostles already insist upon: God shines in places the world calls low.

Hadassah will not trend. She will not be celebrated. But the stakes are real. A child who learns *I can think* is less likely to surrender to chaos. A child who learns *I am seen* is less likely to hunt for belonging in places that devour.

FEEDING IS NOT A METAPHOR ONLY

Teaching participates in the Lord's work. It is not governance of the soul.

You can lay out the path and warn of chasms. You cannot summon rebirth. If you have ever tried to force a miracle, you know how quickly love turns into panic.

Jesus Christ answers cynicism with a shepherd's command: "Feed my lambs" (John 21:15).

Feeding is repetitive. Feeding is costly. Feeding looks small from a distance. Still, it is holy.

And feeding is not only an image. It is Eucharistic logic.

Hadassah slips into the parish chapel some evenings when the building is finally quiet. Fluorescent hallway light gives way to candlelight. She genuflects—more tired than graceful—and sits until her breathing slows. On Sunday she stands shoulder to shoulder with people who will never see her classroom. The Host is lifted—small, white, unremarkable—and the bell rings. "The Body of Christ." Amen. She receives what she cannot produce.

On another day she kneels in a confessional and tells the truth she hates: her impatience, her sharpness, her wish to be done with need. She hears the words she did not earn: *I absolve you.* Mercy, spoken aloud. Her hands are empty when she leaves; that is the point.

Christ gives Himself as Bread, then teaches His body to become what it receives. When the work feels thankless, return to the altar. Let the Cup teach your nervous system what the world refuses to say:

Hidden life matters.
Small faithfulness counts.
Grace is not imaginary.

And in peace-and-justice–shaped Zion language (familiar in Community of Christ), we can name the same reality without triumph: the young are not merely future citizens of the kingdom. They are neighbors now.

Visibility is not a sacrament.

THE MAP THE WORLD DRAWS, AND THE MAP THE KINGDOM USES

We draw maps based on what the world calls "high": status, income, visibility. Then we learn to despise what it calls "low": work that repeats, cleans messes, and forms a soul one choice at a time.

Yet in the kingdom, low places are often where holiness first grows roots.

The work is heavy; the issue is whether the weight is carried with Jesus Christ, in communion with His Church. Burdens carried alone sour into bitterness. Burdens carried with Him become refining—not because they are romantic, but because they are shared.

And because the Lord teaches His people to rest. Jubilees names it with clarity: "Rest, and keep Sabbath from all work on that day" (Jubilees 50:9). Rest is not escape. It is covenant care, a limit that keeps love from turning into resentment. For Catholics, Sunday is a return to the Source. For many Christians across traditions, Sabbath practice becomes obedience shaped by worship.

Hadassah will go home aching, unsure whether any of it mattered. She will stand at the sink and stare too long, fighting the thought that the day was wasted.

Then she will pack her bag anyway.

Tomorrow she will step back into that dust-and-milk room and say "Good morning" to voices. And the Ruach will be there—quietly making room inside a child for light.

Mercy learns a timetable.

PRACTICE

Not grand gestures. Choose one concrete act and complete it.

1. **Bless one teacher with specificity (today).** Send a two-to-three-sentence message naming one observed strength ("I see how you ___"). Add one offer with a date: "I can drop off supplies / lunch on ___." Follow through.

2. **Become a lamp for one child (four weeks).** Choose a rhythm small enough to keep: twenty minutes of reading, a walk, homework help, or a weekly check-in call. Put it on your calendar. Keep it four times. Consistency is mercy with a body.

3. **Refuse contempt out loud (this week).** When someone sneers at children or teachers, don't laugh along. Say one calm sentence: "That work is holy." Then redirect the moment toward gratitude: name someone who carried you when you were hard to love.

The kingdom does not advance by shine. It advances on ordinary faithfulness—love that returns after misunderstanding, and hands that keep feeding the lambs while God does what no classroom can produce: a new heart.

LESSON THREE

Cartography of the Invisible Weight

ZION CANNOT BE BUILT on children trained to disappear inside fear. In Jesus Christ—and in the Church across her long, bruised history—formation is meant to be mercy-shaped: truth without terror, discipline without shame, effort without worship.

Pressure does not begin with exams. It begins earlier, quietly, when a child learns that adults relax when they perform and tighten when they do not. Disappointment gets swallowed fast enough to keep the room calm. Over time, this is renamed *standards*, as if exhaustion were proof of virtue.

But Jesus Christ does not confuse a crushed spirit with a formed one. The Father is not honored by children who learn to smile while they drown. If Zion is ever built, it will not be built on a generation trained to go numb. It will be built the way the kingdom always begins: grace arriving first, love that does not flinch.

If this feels close to home—tiredness, regret, uncertainty—you are not alone.

NOAM AND THE MAPS HE LEARNED TO FOLD

Noam was eight. He loved drawing maps—not the official kind with borders, but maps that refused to behave. Rivers looped backward. Cities floated. In his maps, the world had doors.

At school, doors were not appreciated.

Reading slipped away from him like a bar of soap. Numbers arrived too fast, loud as clanging lockers. When the teacher called on him, his thoughts scattered and his mouth went dry. His fingers pressed into the desk as if he could nail himself to competence.

Adults offered the usual medicine:

Try harder.
Focus.
You have so much potential.

Potential often means: you are almost acceptable—please become easier to manage.

When tests came back, Noam learned to fold the paper quickly and bury it like contraband. At home he answered the daily question with one safe word:

Fine.

It was easier than explaining the ache that followed him from room to room.

One afternoon his father saw the maps on the floor: pencil shavings, eraser crumbs, a small universe spread across the carpet.

"You'll need to take things more seriously," he said. Not cruelly. Just tired. "Life doesn't bend to imagination."

Noam nodded. After his father left, he gathered the pages and redrew his maps smaller and straighter. Something tightened in his chest, like a string pulled and tied.

This is how invisible weight forms: not only through obvious cruelty, but through correction without tenderness—through love made anxious.

The apostle's warning to grown-ups is plain: "Fathers, do not provoke your children to anger . . . but bring them up in the discipline and instruction of the Lord" (Eph 6:4). Discipline that humiliates does not form a soul. It trains a soul to hide.

So Noam learned a survival creed: *If I fail quietly enough, no one will be angry.*

He stopped raising his hand. He stopped drawing the strange maps. Fear is efficient. It produces compliance, not life.

And Jesus Christ did not come to make children compliant. He came to make the weary alive.

A child is not an altar for adult anxiety.

THE INVERSION

Here is the inversion hiding in respectable places: we confuse worth with performance, and formation with pressure. Families, schools, even churches can feel the temptation to love what they can count. They distrust what they cannot score.

But Adonai does not share that addiction to optics: "The LORD does not see as mortals see; they look on the outward appearance, but the LORD looks on the heart" (1 Sam 16:7).

Even older Jewish-rooted witness literature carries an ache that names our danger: "Wisdom went forth to make her dwelling among the children of men, and found no dwelling-place." (1 Enoch 42:2). Not because wisdom was weak, but because hearts can be crowded shut.

So the question is not only how to raise their numbers. It is how to keep their souls from learning despair as doctrine.

Jesus Christ has already entered the rooms where love turns conditional. He has already carried what we keep trying to place on small shoulders. Because He has done that, we are free to learn a different way.

THE MERCY THAT CRACKS THE WEIGHT

One day the class was told, "Draw the world as you see it."

Most children copied atlases. Noam froze. His pencil hovered above the paper.

Do it correctly, the weight whispered.
Don't embarrass yourself.
Don't make this harder.

Then he remembered his old maps: rivers bending backward, floating cities, names that felt like secret prayers. His throat tightened. He hesitated. And then—like stepping off a ledge into water—he began to draw the world that made sense to him.

When the teacher stopped beside his desk, Noam braced for correction.

Instead she asked, quietly, "Tell me about this."

So he did. His voice trembled, and she listened without measuring. No sigh. No sermon. Only attention.

The paper came back later with no grade, only a sentence in the margin: "You see things differently. Don't lose that."

A small mercy cracked the weight.

That is often how the Ruach works: slipping truth into fractures. Giving a child one clean moment where they are not treated as a problem to solve, but a person to know.

A new map began forming in Noam:

- Struggle is not shame.
- Difficulty is not prophecy.
- My worth is not earned by exhaustion.

And that old wisdom-witness still holds: "It is not requisite that a man should run faster than he has strength . . . all things must be done in order" (Mosiah 4:27).

Underneath it—whether Noam could name it yet or not—was the deeper fact:

Jesus Christ sees me.

THE BURDEN THAT IS CARRIED, NOT WORSHIPED

You cannot remove every pressure from a child's life. The world is loud, and it demands offerings. But you can refuse to sanctify the pressure. You can refuse to call anxiety a virtue: "Cast all your anxiety on him, because he cares for you" (1 Pet 5:7).

When His disciples were frayed, Jesus Christ did not tighten the screws. He invited them to withdraw and rest. He is a Shepherd, not a foreman.

Pressure is a false sacrament.

Covenant life matters. But covenant was never meant to be a panic machine. Christ has already kept what we could not keep. So faithfulness becomes quieter:

response,
repair,
return.

Even Jubilees frames formation as direction rather than stopwatch: "The children shall begin to study the laws . . . and to return to the path of righteousness" (Jubilees 23:26). A path, not a timer. Formation, not frenzy.

And the Church knows this in her bones. You can see it on a weekday evening when the line for confession moves slowly—shoes on tile, eyes lowered, someone clutching a worn rosary like a rail. A voice behind the screen. A sentence spoken out loud that finally stops circling in the dark. Then the words you cannot earn: *I absolve you.* Not humiliation. Return.

You can see it on Sunday when the liturgical body stands and kneels together, breath rising and settling, and a small white Host is placed on a tongue that did nothing to deserve it. Communion is not a reward for the unburdened. It is bread for the poor.

So when adults press too hard, the way back is not denial. It is repentance. And repentance looks ordinary: softening the face, loosening the grip, choosing mercy over panic.

A CHARGE TO THE ADULTS WHO LOVE THEM

If you love a child—parent, teacher, leader, older sibling—receive this as invitation:

Do not train children to worship effort.

Effort is good. Discipline can be a gift. But when effort becomes an idol, it eats the soul. Do not let success become a prison and failure a sentence. Teach truth without terror. Offer correction that still leaves room for hope.

A child is not a product. A child is a person—an image-bearer learning to live with mortal limits. They will forget things. They will misunderstand. They will fail.

What they need most is a foundation that does not shift with every grade and every glance: "For no one can lay any foundation other than the one that has been laid; that foundation is Jesus Christ" (1 Cor 3:11).

Noam still carries invisible weight some days. But he no longer believes his life must be crushed to be valuable.

So let no child be trained to extinguish their own flame. You are not manufacturing destiny. You are guarding it. You are building small rooms of Zion inside ordinary weeks, where justice looks like attention and peace looks like repair.

And you are not building alone. Christ builds with you.

Zion grows wherever adults refuse to make love conditional—where discipline is purified of shame, pressure is disentangled from worth, and the child's interior life is guarded as holy ground in communion with Jesus Christ and His Church.

PRACTICE

Small interventions. Real protection.

1. **Name what you see without grading it.** "I notice your kindness." / "I notice how you think." / "I notice how you kept trying." Then stop. Let the naming be enough.
2. **Swap one performance question for a person question.** Instead of "How did you do?" ask, "What felt heavy today?" Listen for two minutes without fixing.
3. **Interrupt "help" that is really pressure.** Before tightening the timetable, pause. Ask Adonai for wisdom. Offer one small choice: "Break first, or start together?"

Pressure starts early. So let it end early, wherever you have power to soften it. A child is more than their score. Worth is not a grade.

Be steady. Be gentle. Keep your hands open. That is how Zion takes root.

LESSON FOUR

Cartography of the Broken Name

DARKNESS IS RARELY CINEMATIC. It is usually ordinary drift. Zion is protected when truth is faced early—confessed in Jesus Christ, with the Church across her histories—where justice and mercy are held together and repentance becomes concrete in the light.

We prefer villains tidy. Prepackaged monsters keep evil far enough away to point at, recoil from, and feel clean. But real darkness is often banal. It says *I'm fine* and learns to sound believable.

If you are already tired—tired of hard truths, tired of holding your life together—hear this once: this is not entertainment. It is a mirror. But it is a mirror held by mercy.

Jesus Christ has already stepped into the places we avoid. Because He took sin seriously on the Cross, we do not have to perform "fine" in order to be loved. The Unseen Father sees what we hide: "For God will bring every deed into judgment, including every secret thing, whether good or evil" (Eccl 12:14).

He sees now, not to humiliate, but to call us into truth while truth can still heal. *Confession is mercy before collapse.* One of the most dangerous lies is believing you cannot be redeemed.

TOMAS AND THE SLOW UNMAKING

The man in this telling has a name. We will call him Tomas.

He grew up where love existed but ran thin—money short, arguments common, tenderness occasional. He learned early that being "good" sometimes meant being invisible. He learned to take up less space.

Sin rarely kicks the door in. It waits, then offers relief: *Just this once. Just to get through.*

Tomas was spoken over with sacred language—calling, service, destiny. Some of it was sincere. Some of it was fear dressed as guidance. A path can be good and still be forced, and forced belief bruises where it should bless.

So Tomas ran into the in-between: work without meaning, reinvention attempts, outrunning a shame that already knew his name. Some evenings he sat in his car with the engine off and felt a thought rise like pressure in the chest: *This cannot be all I am.*

Then debt arrived. Debt becomes leverage: "The rich rule over the poor, and the borrower is the slave of the lender" (Prov 22:7).

The man who held Tomas's debt was polished. Cruelty rarely announces itself. It calls itself "how the world works," and smiles while it takes.

Inside Tomas, hope began to rot—not his ability, but his belief that turning back would matter. From the outside he still looked ordinary. Inside, one thought returned like a drumbeat: *Nothing I do matters. I'm already finished.*

When a person believes that, temptation does not need to look beautiful. It only needs to look like relief.

One night Tomas crossed a threshold he could not uncross. A human life was taken by his hand.

I will not make this a scene. The point is the fracture: after violence, the self you relied on begins to split. Tomas felt it—like standing in a familiar room and suddenly not recognizing the furniture.

This does not absolve Tomas. He is guilty. Consequences matter. The victim matters. Grief matters. Justice is not optional, and mercy is not denial.

But the descent matters too, because it teaches us what to watch for *before* the next fall. If all we believe is "some people are monsters," we will miss ordinary unraveling. We will also miss the chance to intervene while confession is still possible.

EXPOSURE AND THE HARD MERCY OF TRUTH

After the act came the scramble to paste normality over memory. But hidden things rise: "Nothing is covered up that will not be uncovered, and nothing secret that will not become known" (Luke 12:2).

Exposure is not always vengeance. Sometimes it is mercy wearing a hard face—the last chance to stop pretending.

When Tomas was found out, the world split fast. Some wanted punishment without mercy. Others wanted mercy without consequence. Neither is the way of Jesus Christ.

Christ does not flatter the guilty or erase the wounded. He holds truth without hatred, and mercy without pretending. Repentance is not an escape hatch. It is the only road that does not end in ash.

Many hear *repentance* and assume it means humiliation. In the gospel, repentance is a doorway. The Shepherd calls His sheep out of the ravine not to mock them, but to carry them home.

Despair is not repentance. It is a verdict spoken too early.

Jubilees names the mercy without sentiment: "If they turn to him . . . He will forgive . . . and pardon" (Jubilees 5:17). The point is not permission. The point is this: *Guilt is not God.*

And from the Restoration witness, I still keep Alma's cry as a clean line of truth: "O Jesus, thou Son of God, have mercy on me," and then, "Oh, what joy" (Alma 36:18–19). Mercy is asked for, not manufactured.

In Catholic life—and alongside other ancient Christian practices of confession, counsel, and accountability—that cry is given somewhere to land: not an idea, but a place. A quiet room. A screen or a chair. A stole. A voice that does not gasp when the sin is named. Truth spoken aloud, without theater; penance received as medicine. Not to cancel justice, but to begin conversion in the light.

THE BROKEN NAME

At the center of many collapses is not one appetite, but one belief: *My name is ruined.*

Once you accept that, sin becomes easier. Honesty becomes harder. Confession feels pointless. The Accuser whispers, *You might as well become what you fear you are.*

Tomas believed his name was broken long before the crime. The crime began in interior surrender.

This is why labels are dangerous. A story repeated often enough becomes a prison, and prisons rarely produce repentance. They produce hiding.

The Unseen Father names sin as sin, and does not reduce a soul to its worst act. He offers forgiveness and cleansing: "If we confess our sins, he who is faithful and just will forgive us our sins and cleanse us from all unrighteousness" (1 John 1:9).

Some harms cannot be repaired in mortality. Atonement is not erasing history. Yet the miracle remains: Jesus Christ can change what history tries to make you. *A broken name is not a final name.*

Enoch speaks in the language of record and remembrance: "Your names are written before the glory of the Great One. . . .Be hopeful . . . now ye shall shine as the lights of heaven" (1 Enoch 108:1–2). Hopeful, not excused. Hopeful, not hidden. Hopeful, because God's mercy is not fragile.

WARNINGS HIDDEN INSIDE THE STORY

Watch for drift before disaster: the hollow stare, the forced laugh, the sudden withdrawal, the moment someone starts believing they are beyond help.

Intervene early with presence and burden-bearing: "Bear one another's burdens, and in this way you will fulfill the law of Christ" (Gal 6:2).

Hold the plumb line.

- Do not feed the mob, because *hatred is not holiness.*
- Do not feed denial, because vagueness is not mercy.
- Zion is not built by cruelty, and it is not protected by pretending.

The Church must be especially honest here. Where she has failed to protect, she must repent concretely: truth told, harm named, the vulnerable safeguarded, justice pursued without spectacle. Institutional humility is not silence. It is fidelity.

Peace-and-justice–shaped streams of Christian life (including Community of Christ instincts) often name the same discipline: accountability without vengeance, healing without denial, mercy that refuses both hatred and hiding.

If you are reading this with a knot in your stomach—thinking of someone you love, or thinking of yourself—do not waste that sensation by baptizing it as shame. It may be alarm. It may be mercy.

WHAT TO DO WHEN YOU FEEL DRIFT IN YOURSELF

Drift is closer than we like to admit: hiding, numbing, smoothing justification. The broken-name lie tempts faithful people too: *You've failed too much. You don't belong.*

If you feel drift, do not wait for collapse to force honesty. Turn now. Tell the truth now. Ask for help now.

Confess to the Unseen Father, and when needed bring your truth into the light with a trusted priest, pastor, counselor, or wise elder who can walk with you. If there is immediate danger to you or to someone else, seek urgent help through local emergency services and qualified professionals. Mercy does not mean managing disaster alone.

The Unseen Father does not heal what we insist on hiding. And because Jesus Christ has already carried the weight of our sin, we are free to step into the light without pretending we can save ourselves.

THE NAME THE SAVIOR GIVES

Repentance is new creation: "So if anyone is in Christ, there is a new creation: everything old has passed away; see, everything has become new!" (2 Cor 5:17).

Courts can sentence. They cannot resurrect. Resurrection belongs to Jesus Christ.

Zion is built when people refuse both hatred and hiding—when sin is named without spectacle, victims are honored without being used, and the broken-name lie is answered by concrete repentance in the light of Christ and His Church.

PRACTICE

Small steps. Real light.

1. **Refuse the cartoon-villain story (write it).** In a notebook, write two sentences:
   - "Darkness often begins as drift."
   - "I will not wait until collapse to tell the truth."
2. **Tend one small wound (within forty-eight hours).** Message one person who seems to be dimming: "You've seemed quieter lately. I care about you. Do you want a walk or a call this week?" Then follow up once if they don't reply.
3. **Hold truth without hatred (one concrete act).** Pray once, out loud: "Unseen Father, keep me from cruelty and from denial. Give me courage to turn." Then choose one light-bearing action: go to confession this week and name the sin plainly; set one accountability conversation; or book one counseling appointment.

Zion is protected when we stop feeding darkness in secret and start walking in truth—early, concretely, and without theatrics—because the Light has already gone into the ordinary rooms where we are afraid to speak.

LESSON FIVE

Cartography of the Hearth Under Judgment

Discipleship doesn't stay sanctuary-sound. It proves itself at the hearth—where scarcity and stewardship collide, where need arrives without appointment, where neighbor-love is either practiced or postponed. Mercy is not an idea. Mercy is edible.

Ordinary rooms tell the truth faster than chapels. A chapel can feel holy while a heart stays hidden. A study can sound wise while hands stay closed. There is one room where theology refuses to remain theory because someone has to eat.

It is the kitchen.

Here, belief becomes groceries. What we confess—Father, Son, and Holy Spirit—is tested by what we do with bread, leftovers, and the knock at the door. Adonai reads souls in pantries and at tables. "Oppressing the poor in order to enrich oneself, and giving to the rich, will lead only to loss" (Prov 22:16).

Jesus Christ came near to hunger. He does not let us spiritualize it away.

From the Restoration road that shaped my early moral imagination, I still carry this as a plain standard: after hope in Christ, "ye will seek [riches] for to do good—to clothe the naked, and to feed the hungry" (Jacob 2:19). Not as a riddle. As a measure of whether love has become real.

LEAH AND THE POT THAT REFUSES TO AGREE WITH HER PURSE

Leah lives in a cramped flat. Her kitchen is barely a room: a stove that clicks before it catches, one tired light, a tap that runs cold too long.

She stands at the stove with a pot and a problem. The money in her hand and the food in her pot no longer agree.

Avi, her son, sits at the table with his feet swinging, pretending he is not watching her count. "Is there meat tonight?" he asks, casual in the way children are casual when they already know.

"Not much," Leah says. "But there will be enough."

She says it like a prayer dressed as a sentence. She has learned the mathematics of mercy: slice the carrots thinner, stretch the broth, save the better portion for the child, smile as if it costs nothing.

Because she is tired, temptation comes in whispers that sound like wisdom: *If I had been wiser. If the world were kinder. If God were closer.* If you have stood in front of a refrigerator and felt your hope thin out, you know this place. Not dramatic. Just heavy.

Scripture names how suffering is sustained by choices made far away from the people who pay for them: "The wages of the laborers . . . which you kept back by fraud, cry out" (James 5:4). Leah has no time for theories. She has time for the shop, then the stove, then the last week of the month.

At the market she recalculates, moving items in and out of the basket as if rearranging them might rearrange reality. The total appears too high. She removes an item, pays, and leaves with less than she intended.

Outside, she passes wealth in shop windows, an ad promising ease, a man asking for spare change. Bitterness rises—quick and almost comforting—then she climbs the stairs and returns to the one place where bitterness must become something else because a child is waiting.

She fills the pot. The smell of onions and garlic warms the room. She slices the meat so thin it almost disappears, tastes, adjusts the salt, and prays without forming words: *Please. Let this be enough. And if it is not, do not let my son feel it.*

Mercy has a weight. It usually sits in a pot.

THE HEARTH IS WHERE DISCIPLESHIP GETS HONEST

Comfortable religion can act as if "spiritual" needs are the only ones that matter. Jesus Christ never taught that. He fed crowds. He dignified hunger without shaming it. "Your heavenly Father knows that you need all these things" (Matt 6:32).

Need is not a scandal to Adonai.

The Holy One does not despise matter. He meets us in it: bread, water, a table, a body strengthened enough to try again tomorrow.

And Catholic life makes this unavoidable. On Sunday, the line forms. Shoes scuff the tile. A mother hushes a child. An old man steadies himself on the pew. The priest lifts the Host—small as a coin, heavy as a world—and places it into open hands. *The Body of Christ. Amen.* We swallow heaven and then walk back into our week with mouths still tasting wheat.

If the Church is Christ's body, bodies matter. If the bread is truly received, it teaches our hands what we have received. Gratitude becomes generosity. Worship becomes stewardship. "The earth is the LORD's and all that is in it" (Ps 24:1).

If the world is His, then "not enough" is not always private failure. Sometimes it is injustice. Sometimes it is the revealed shape of our love: what we protect, what we excuse, who we allow to become invisible.

Jubilees names the wound without softening it: the poor and the rich torn apart "on account of the law and the covenant" (Jubilees 23:19). Covenant neglect becomes neighbor neglect. The gospel does not excuse us from this. It drags our prayers into the light.

YOSEF AND THE QUIET HOLINESS OF INTERRUPTION

Across the hall lives Yosef—not rich, but awake.

He notices Leah's laughter flattening. He sees bags that are too light. He hears, through thin walls, the silence that comes when a parent is doing math they do not want a child to learn.

One evening there is a knock. Leah opens the door bracing for a complaint.

Yosef holds out a loaf of bread, still warm enough to fog the plastic, and a small bag with two onions.

"Bought too much," he says.

"I can't—" Leah begins, pride and fear braided together.

"Yes you can," he replies, gentle and final. "Take it before it goes bad."

He turns and walks away. He does not linger. He does not demand a performance of gratitude. He makes room for her dignity by refusing to turn mercy into theater.

Leah stands there with bread in hand, and something loosens. Not triumph. Not even relief. A quiet undoing: *Heaven saw me.* Not because bread fell from the sky, but because a neighbor agreed to become the Lord's hands.

The Ruach often moves like this—by interruption that refuses to let hunger isolate a soul.

THE FAST THAT TURNS KITCHENS INTO ZION

Fasting is not display. It is a discipline that will not let faith stay abstract. It unmasks what rules us, and if it is true, it turns outward into bread for someone else.

"Is it not to share your bread with the hungry . . . and not to hide yourself . . .?" (Isa 58:7). The fast Adonai desires is not mainly what you refuse. It is what you give.

The world draws one map of worth: profit, power, distance, efficiency. The gospel draws another: stewardship, presence, mercy, shared bread. Enoch names the seduction without politeness:

"Woe to you, rich, for you have trusted in your riches" (1 Enoch 94:8).

And Jesus Christ leaves us with a test simple enough to frighten us: "I was hungry and you gave me food. . . . I was a stranger and you welcomed me" (Matt 25:35).

Bring discipleship to the stove, the cupboard, the table. The Unseen Father does not ask you to feed the world. He asks you not to walk past Leah. He asks you to become the kind of person who notices.

Zion takes root when Eucharistic logic becomes lived logic: gifts received with gratitude, then translated into concrete mercy—until kitchens stop being places of quiet shame and become places where no one is treated as invisible.

If you can say *Amen* to the Bread, you can learn to share bread.

PRACTICE

Choose one small act and complete it quietly.

1. **Sanctify your ordinary (today).** Before you eat one meal, say aloud, "Unseen Father, this table is Yours." Pause for ten seconds. Let gratitude become confession: *I am held.*
2. **Turn fasting into food (this week).** Skip one comfort purchase. Give the exact amount you saved to a food bank, a struggling neighbor, or a mutual-aid fund. No announcement. Make love edible.
3. **Refuse distance (within seven days).** Learn one name behind an "issue." A neighbor, a volunteer, a parent at the school gate, a person you usually pass by. Use their name once, pray for them once, then do one concrete thing: a loaf, a lift, a bag of groceries, a message that opens a door.

Zion is not an idea. Zion is mercy that shows up where onions sizzle and dishes stack—and keeps showing up until the table is no longer lonely.

LESSON SIX

Cartography of the Breathing Sabbath

SABBATH IS NOT COLLAPSE after overwork. It is covenant time that teaches belonging before productivity. In the Name of the Father, Son, and Holy Spirit, rest becomes steadiness, not escape.

We treat rest like recovery for the machine we've become. Then we try to press it like a button: mark a day, close the shops, expect peace to arrive on schedule. But exhaustion is not that polite.

You can keep a day off and still feel hunted, because the noise is not only around you. It is inside you.

From the beginning, Scripture offers a rhythm older than our frantic timetables: God blesses the seventh day and hallows it (Gen 2:3). Adonai sets apart time to teach what our age resists: you belong before you produce. In Jesus Christ, that belonging is not a prize at the end of your effort. It is given while you are still tired. Sabbath trains the body in that truth through the one language you cannot avoid: time.

Sabbath is belonging, measured in hours.

DANIEL AND THE COUNTERFEIT SABBATHS

Daniel works in a warehouse where the lights hum and scanners never stop beeping. The air smells like cardboard and machine oil. His hands learn the weight of things that are not his, and his spine memorizes strain.

Daniel is not lazy. He is worn. Some evenings he can't tell whether what he feels is anger, sadness, or the dull throb of surviving.

When the week loosens its grip, the world offers him rest. Often it offers substitution.

One counterfeit Sabbath is enforced stillness. Daniel sits in his apartment and learns that silence is not automatically peace. He checks his phone, puts it down, picks it up again. He paces.

Another counterfeit Sabbath is distraction: streaming, scrolling, brightness that pretends to be relief. He insists he is relaxing while his pulse stays high and his mind stays crowded.

Scripture speaks of rest as more than the absence of labor. "So the land had rest forty years" (Judg 3:11). That is steadiness, not an afternoon. And Isaiah names the shape of it: "In returning and rest you shall be saved; in quietness and in trust shall be your strength" (Isa 30:15). Rest is received before it is achieved.

Because Jesus Christ has already carried what crushes us, quiet does not have to be manufactured by willpower. It can be entered.

THE CHAIN THAT PRETENDS TO BE COMFORT

Daniel's ache reaches for something that looks like mercy. It starts small: just for tonight, just to sleep, just to stop thinking. At first it seems harmless. Then it becomes familiar. Then it becomes necessary—not because it gives joy, but because it gives numbness.

Numbness is not rest.

This is the cruelty of counterfeit comfort: it does not lift you into life. It lowers you into a place you start calling normal.

Jesus Christ does not invite the weary into oblivion. He says, "Come to me . . . and I will give you rest" (Matt 11:28). Rest with a face. Rest that carries you without erasing you.

When the substitute becomes a chain, mercy becomes practical. Bring it into confession where that is your practice. Bring it into honest help—pastoral, clinical, communal—so you are not fighting alone. The Church is meant to be a body, not an audience.

LIBERATION, NOT COLLAPSE

Sabbath was never meant to be "work until you fray, then collapse into one misused day." The commandment is tied to liberation: "Remember that you were a slave in the land of Egypt" (Deut 5:15). The Father does not call you to be a machine. He calls you to be a person—beloved before useful.

Jesus Christ says it plainly: "The sabbath was made for humankind, and not humankind for the sabbath" (Mark 2:27).

Even Jewish-rooted witness literature keeps its weight. Jubilees calls Sabbath a "great sign" (Jubilees 2:17)—not a badge, but a signpost pointing home.

THE SABBATH THAT BREATHES

A breathing Sabbath is not a perfect schedule. It is a posture of return, time set apart to remember what you forget all week:

- God is real.
- You are more than your output.
- The Ruach can quiet a human heart.
- Covenant people are meant to carry one another.

It is not simply *not doing*. It is returning.

Isaiah dares to name it: "Call the sabbath a delight" (Isa 58:13). Not because life is easy, but because you are no longer alone inside it.

So make it concrete.

Daniel shaves, not to impress, but to show up. He steps into the nave with the week still clinging to him. He stands when the people stand. He kneels when they kneel. He hears the Scriptures read aloud—words that do not hurry. He says, with everyone else, "Lord, I am not worthy," and still holds out his hands.

The Host is placed there like a refusal of the ranking system. Gift, not wage.

Later—another day, another kind of courage—he sits in the small room, tells the truth without decoration, and hears words that do not flatter and do not crush: *I absolve you.* Mercy with a spine.

Worship re-centers. Communion remembers. Confession unties what secrecy cinches tight. A people learns again that God is not a taskmaster.

Daniel doesn't realize how loud his life has become until he sits among the people of God and feels something clean: not condemnation, invitation. Jeremiah's map returns: "Stand at the crossroads, . . . ask for the ancient paths, . . . and find rest for your souls" (Jer 6:16).

REST THAT TURNS OUTWARD

Sabbath is not a private luxury. Grace turns outward.

Because Jesus Christ gives rest you did not earn, you are freed—slowly—to become shelter for someone else. James gives a simple test: "Religion that is pure and undefiled . . . is this: to care for orphans and widows in their distress" (Jas 1:27).

Zion is not what you build to prove devotion. Zion is what rest looks like when it becomes a people—when mercy gains hands and feet. Peace-and-justice instincts, so present in Community of Christ's moral imagination, name this without triumph: rest that does not hoard comfort, but makes room for the neighbor.

A SMALL PORTION OF HOLY GROUND

In Daniel's life it begins smaller than he expects: a daily portion of holy ground.

Sleep without guilt. Silence without performance. Prayer without lists. Scripture without rushing. A walk without destination. A meal without a screen. A phone turned off long enough for your mind to remember it has its own voice.

One night he comes home tired and reaches for the old substitute. His hand pauses—not because he becomes heroic, but because he remembers invitation. He opens a window. Cold air enters. He sits with empty hands.

For a moment, nothing "spiritual" happens. Then, quietly, something unclenches: "For he gives sleep to his beloved" (Ps 127:2).

Sabbath is not only a day. It is a direction. Daniel's life does not instantly become easy. He still has work, bills, habits to unlearn. Some days he fumbles. But he is turning—and Jesus Christ is patient with turning.

The breathing Sabbath is how Christ retrains a frantic life: rest received in worship and communion, practiced in small daily returns, and proven by mercy that turns outward—until the body remembers its true name.

Beloved.

PRACTICE

Make it small enough to keep.

1. **Defend ten minutes daily (seven days).** Set a timer. No screens. Sit, walk, breathe, pray one sentence ("Unseen Father, receive me"), or read six to ten verses. When the timer ends, stop.
2. **Let rest turn outward once (this week).** Choose one act that fits your limits: a call, a doorstep meal, a lift, childcare for an hour, or quiet practical help. Put it on a specific day. Do it.
3. **Trade one counterfeit comfort for a true one (tonight).** Pick one: sleep thirty minutes earlier, drink water, take a slow walk, read one psalm, sit in silence for five minutes, or play one hymn. Do it without multitasking.

Sabbath is not a badge. It is a door. Step through without hurry.

LESSON SEVEN

Cartography of the Unfinished Name

A NAME DOES NOT retire.

In the Name of the Father, and of the Son, and of the Holy Spirit, no one is "used up." The Church confesses a God who carries what the world discards. Zion becomes visible when elders are honored as kin, not managed as projects.

It's easy to believe the paycheck is the last proof you mattered. Retirement as vanishing. Aging as apology. "Being a burden," as if a soul were a line item.

Heaven does not speak that way.

The Unseen Father does not confuse output with worth. Jesus Christ does not measure a life by speed. He walked at human pace. He received fatigue. He carried weakness to the Cross. The Resurrection is His refusal to let anyone be renamed as useful—or used up.

Enoch speaks like a door held open: "Hear, ye men of old time . . . and see, ye that come after" (1 Enoch 37:2). The old and the coming-after belong to one story, held in one mercy.

MARA AND REUBEN

Mara is nine—old enough to notice everything, young enough to say it plainly.

Her school hosts Grandparents Day. Paper flowers are taped to the walls. The gym smells like warm butter and biscuits. Mara brings her grandfather, Reuben.

He arrives early because rushing costs him. His coat is old because money is. His hands stay folded in his lap, as if he's practicing how to take up less space.

Mara reads what she wrote: how Reuben taught her cards, how his stories open windows, how his laugh is real. His eyes shine. For a moment his shoulders loosen—like someone has spoken his name out loud and meant it.

Then snacks.

Reuben drifts to the edge. He has learned what happens when he stands too close to food: pity arrives dressed as management. He would rather be hungry than handled.

Mara walks over and puts half her biscuit into his hand, casual as breath. He freezes—not from ingratitude, but recognition. Children give without calculation. Adults often give after bargaining with fear.

"Grandpa," she says, "why don't you eat with everyone else?"

"I'm not hungry," he answers too fast.

"You always say that," she says. "But your fridge is empty."

The room keeps moving. The sentence doesn't.

THE ENVELOPE

Later, at Reuben's flat, Mara sees an envelope on the table—creased, official. Reuben glances away like the paper can accuse him.

"It's nothing," he says.

Mara tilts her head. "Why does it make you sad?"

He exhales. "This is what I get. It used to be enough."

Mara frowns, as if the world has broken a rule. "But you didn't get worse. Why did it stop being enough?"

"Things cost more," he says. "The paper stayed the same."

"That's cheating," she says—small voice, heavy truth.

Leviticus doesn't make honor optional: "You shall rise before the aged" (Lev 19:32). Reverence for elders is welded to reverence for God.

And Jesus Christ refuses to let it stay abstract. Even on the Cross, He secured care for His mother (John 19:26–27). Grace first—then a shape, then a cost.

Jubilees says it without ornament: "Honour father and mother, and love thy neighbour" (Jubilees 7:20).

When a society worships loudly while elders thin their meals into survival, heaven names the sin.

THE LIE BENEATH THE LABELS

We answer old age with contempt or sentimentality.

Contempt calls elders obsolete and calls that efficiency. Sentimentality posts quotes and celebrates birthdays while leaving loneliness untouched. Both kneel before the same god: worth is what you produce.

The psalmist prays like someone who has felt the room turn away: "Do not cast me off . . . when my strength is spent" (Ps 71:9). And Isaiah gives a promise you can lean your weight on: "To gray hairs I will carry you" (Isa 46:4).

If God carries the gray-haired, discipleship cannot be a sprint-only faith. A Church that cannot carry the slow has forgotten its Shepherd.

If "not enough" shows up at an elder's table, tell the truth about it. Sometimes it's misfortune. Sometimes it's structural. Either way, the Church is not permitted to look away.

WHEN HEAVEN REFUSES TO LET A NAME SHRINK

That night Mara asks in the kitchen, loud as a bell, "Why is Grandpa's fridge empty?"

Her mother flinches—not from lack of love, but from shame, money, and the fear of not having enough. She returns later with groceries, trying to make it casual.

Reuben accepts with a practiced smile, then stares at the bags as if they are both mercy and humiliation. He hates needing. He hates being seen.

Honor is not sentiment. It is bread without humiliation.

On Sunday, Reuben comes to Mass. He moves slowly down the aisle. Knees complain. The congregation stands anyway—not as theater, as obedience. The body breathes together: standing, sitting, kneeling, rising again. At the altar rail, Reuben opens his hands like a man relearning how to receive.

"The Body of Christ."

"Amen."

No speech. No spotlight. Just covenant made edible.

Later that week a leader from the congregation visits Reuben and does not begin with fixes. He asks how Reuben is sleeping, what feels heavy, what hurts that no one notices. He doesn't rush. The room becomes safe.

Eventually Reuben whispers, "I'm tired of counting coins."

A door opens—help with steadiness, not spectacle. A small plan that can be kept. Then the visitor asks, gently, "Would you help with something?"

A younger man in the community needs someone steady. "Would you talk with him sometimes?"

Reuben hesitates, then nods.

The world has been trying to rename him as useless. The Lord refuses.

Malachi names the covenant motion: hearts turned toward one another (Mal 4:6). Turning hearts looks like slowing down to their tempo, listening without treating their stories as filler, removing humiliations where we can.

THE UNFINISHED NAME

A week later Mara arrives with a notebook. "I want to write your stories," she says, "so they don't disappear."

Reuben tells her about work, love, failure, survival. His voice shakes once; he clears his throat like he's embarrassed to be human.

Then she asks, "What do you want people to remember?"

He says, very small, "That I tried."

Mara shakes her head. "That's not enough. You're still you."

Yes.

Your worth is not a season. Your name does not end because the room got quieter. Heaven is still speaking it.

Jarom holds the duty in plain words: "Watch over" souls with diligence (Jarom 1:11). Not control. Not pressure. A refusal to let a person drift into disappearance.

Jubilees blesses what the world neglects: "May thy name and thy seed endure" (Jubilees 25:21). Enoch sees the end as belonging: "The dwelling-places of the holy . . . the resting-places of the righteous" (1 Enoch 39:4). Not shelving. Not vanishing. Resting-places.

If you fear you only matter when you are productive, bring that fear to Jesus Christ. He dismantles it without shaming you. Grace comes first. Covenant love follows.

Zion refuses usefulness as its god. It honors elders as image-bearers with unfinished callings, removes humiliations with quiet fidelity, and makes intergenerational communion visible proof that the Resurrection has redefined what "a life well-lived" means.

PRACTICE

Small commitments you can actually keep.

1. **Stand and slow down (this week).** Schedule thirty minutes with one elder. Ask one question that can't be answered quickly:
    - "What was hard about your twenties?"
    - "What do you wish people understood about you now?"

Put your phone away. Don't multitask.

2. **Remove one humiliation (within seven days).** Choose one concrete burden and take it off their hands: groceries, a lift, a bill sorted, a prescription collected, a small repair arranged. Do it quietly—then repeat it once next week.
3. **Refuse usefulness as your god (once, deliberately).** Spend time with someone who cannot advance your life. No networking. No moral theater. Bring one practical offering: a meal, a walk, a listening ear, a ride, or help with one task.

Zion is not a slogan. It is a people who refuse to let the vulnerable become invisible—especially when the world insists their names should be finished. Speak the name. Set the chair. Let the Ruach supply what you lack, and let your care become the map.

LESSON EIGHT

Cartography of the Carried Ascent

HOLINESS IS NOT A ladder climbed by the strong. Nearness is given by Jesus Christ, received in communion, and carried by grace—until Zion becomes the kind of community where there is room for breath, slowness, and the fragile.

Many of us love ladders: steps, systems, "next stages." The proud part of the soul finds a punishing climb oddly comforting. If holiness is a summit and salvation looks like discipline, we can quietly imagine we earned our view.

Even Scripture can be misread into ladder-religion: "Who shall ascend the hill of the LORD? And who shall stand in his holy place?" (Ps 24:3). It is easy to picture burning legs, as if righteousness were a fitness test and God were timing our pace.

But the psalm does not praise stamina. It asks who is clean enough to come near. The answer is not a training plan. It is a heart: "Those who have clean hands and pure hearts" (Ps 24:4).

Clean hands are not purchased by grind. They grow where repentance meets mercy—where we turn toward Jesus Christ and let Him change what willpower cannot. Because Christ has already come down to us—Incarnation, not distance—we are free to stop pretending we can climb our way into love.

Ladder-religion has one doctrine: *the strong belong closer*. It can sound devout. It turns good news into a gate. It makes weakness feel like disqualification.

Adonai breaks that spell by drawing near to those who want God and cannot pay the entry fee of strength. And the Church, across her histories, keeps repeating the same steady truth: nearness is gift before it is effort.

ALON AND THE HILL THAT DEMANDED TOO MUCH

Alon is ten. A heart condition turns steep stairs into a negotiation with panic. In winter air his breath goes thin too fast, and he hates how quickly his body tells the truth. He watches other kids sprint and laughs along like it does not sting.

He loves chapels, though—not because he understands everything, but because they feel like places where the world hushes itself. Places where it might be safe to be small.

In his town an old meetinghouse sits on a hill. Each year they keep a dawn walk: flashlights in the dark, cocoa in paper cups, a hymn sung too early for anyone's voice to be warm. They call it devotion.

Alon calls it dread.

He starts anyway, holding his mother's hand and smiling like he is fine. The hill rises the way rules rise when compassion is not invited into the sentence.

Halfway up, his chest tightens. Breath turns sharp. His mother slows.

"It's okay," Alon lies, because somewhere along the way he learned a cruel theology: love means not becoming a burden.

A man behind them laughs—not unkindly, just careless. "Come on, it's not that steep."

Alon's face burns. He looks up. The meetinghouse sits at the top like a promise. Fear puts on a halo: *Don't ruin this. Don't make them turn back.*

His mother kneels, wipes sweat from his forehead, and whispers, "We can go back."

"No," Alon says, and his voice shakes. "I want to be there."

His problem is not laziness. His problem is not desire. His problem is that he is human.

Most of us don't name our limits as "a heart condition." We call them failure.

SISTER ILARIA AND THE ROAD BUILT FOR MERCY

A woman named Ilaria finds them. She is a nurse—steady hands, clear eyes—the calm of someone who knows mercy is not a mood. It is a decision.

She kneels beside Alon and begins with dignity, not pity. "Do you want to be up there?"

He nods, swallowing hard.

She points toward an old service road that curves around the hill. It's for deliveries and repairs, the path no one brags about because it doesn't make a clean story.

"I can take you up this way," she says.

Alon's cheeks tighten. "That's cheating."

"No," she answers. "That's mercy."

The road loops instead of climbs. Alon's breathing steadies. The hill still rises, but it no longer demands that nearness must be purchased with pain.

At the doors, the group is already inside. The air smells faintly of old wood and cocoa. Prayers sound like morning.

Alon steps into the hush and whispers—half confession, half wonder—"I didn't climb like them . . . but I'm here."

Mercy is not cheating.
If the gospel is true, that sentence is closer to worship than any bragging ascent.

From the Restoration road that shaped my early language of hope, I still keep this promise of welcome: "Come unto me, ye blessed, there is a place prepared for you" (Enos 1:27).

WHAT THE CARRIED ASCENT EXPOSES

When we speak of "ascent," two temptations arrive.

One is the worship of difficulty. Pain becomes proof. The strong feel superior while still calling it devotion.

The other is avoidance. Retreat gets renamed "discernment," and loneliness gets renamed peace.

Both keep the self in control.

Jesus Christ offers something else: "Come to me, all you that are weary and are carrying heavy burdens, and I will give you rest" (Matt 11:28). And He presses the point: "For my yoke is easy, and my burden is light" (Matt 11:30).

Light does not mean imaginary. It means the weight is carried by Someone stronger than you.

The Unseen Father does not stand on the ridge shouting instructions. He comes down into the ravine and takes the load. The Cross is not a metaphor. It is the place where mercy became flesh—where Christ carried what we could not carry, up a real hill, with real lungs, for real people who cannot make themselves clean.

Grace doesn't say, *Climb faster.*
It says, *Let Me carry you.*

"My grace is sufficient for you, for power is made perfect in weakness" (2 Cor 12:9).

THE WAY IS A PERSON, NOT A SYSTEM

You do not ascend to the Father through a program. You come through a Person: "I am the way, and the truth, and the life" (John 14:6).

Because Jesus Christ has opened the way, covenant life becomes response rather than ransom—God sanctifying a people for Himself.

Jubilees names the direction: "I will separate unto Myself a people . . . and I will sanctify them . . . and they shall be My people and I will be their God" (Jubilees 2:19). The engine is not our climb. It is God's claim.

And this is not private. It takes a body.

A line forms. Knees creak. Hands open. The Host is lifted—*The Body of Christ*—and the weak are not asked for credentials. They are fed.

Later, in a quiet side chapel, someone stumbles through the truth they were hiding. The priest listens without shock. The words land like a door unbolting: *I absolve you. . . .* And what was heavy becomes carryable again.

This is how the Church makes the service road real: not a shortcut around holiness, but mercy given shape so the weak can arrive without shame.

NOT PUNISHING WEAKNESS

Ladder-religion treats limitation as moral failure. But the Servant is named by what He refuses to crush: "A bruised reed he will not break" (Isa 42:3).

So Zion learns different questions.

Not: Who deserves it?
But: Who needs help arriving?

"Bear one another's burdens, and in this way you will fulfill the law of Christ" (Gal 6:2).

The map of a holy people is not drawn by the strong showing off altitude. It is drawn by a community that makes room—for breath, for slowness, for the fragile—because Jesus Christ has made room for us.

That is covenant ethics.
That is lived discipleship.
That is Zion.

THE CARRIED ASCENT BECOMES ZION

Alon's condition does not vanish. But he learns that access to the sustaining Ruach is not reserved for the strong.

He returns. Some days he takes the steep path for a stretch. Some days the service road is the whole way. But he arrives. Each arrival disciples him out of shame.

Enoch speaks of the righteous being given a place of life, not a prize for the elite: "A division has been made . . . for the spirits of the righteous, in which there is the bright spring of water" (1 Enoch 22:9–10).

So let your ladders fall. Let mercy be the map. Jesus Christ does not despise the pace of the human heart.

Zion is mercy made structural.
And the ones who arrive slowly still arrive beloved.

PRACTICE

Make it embodied and specific.

1. **Take the service road on purpose (this week).** Choose one place you usually "push through" to prove something. Take the gentler route instead: arrive ten minutes early, sit when you need to sit, ask for help once, or choose the accessible option without apology. Write one sentence afterward: "Mercy is not cheating."
2. **Refuse to punish weakness (within seven days).** Do one concrete accommodation for someone: offer a seat, slow the pace, give a ride, shorten the walk, adjust the plan, check in afterward. Do it without commentary.
3. **Let Jesus Christ set the pace (today).** Stop bargaining with God through effort for one prayer. Say, "Unseen Father, I come as I am." Then receive one small gift of grace: five minutes of silence, one psalm, one decade of the Rosary, one hymn, or one simple confession spoken plainly.

Zion is built by a people who make sure the fragile can arrive—because they trust the One who carries the ascent all the way home.

LESSON NINE

Cartography of the Counted Shadows

Counting can be a kind of mercy. It can also be a kind of erasure.

You can be counted and still unseen. A number beside your name is not recognition. Sometimes it is inventory—the way a warehouse notices boxes.

In Jesus Christ—confessed with the Church in the Name of the Father, and of the Son, and of the Holy Spirit—names are held for communion, not control. The counted are meant to be seen.

And yes, the temptation to count is real. When life keeps happening without asking permission—people moving, children arriving, rent rising, needs multiplying—anxiety whispers: we are losing control. So machinery does what machinery does. It sends forms.

Some counting is necessary. Bodies need food. Bills need paying. Communities need to know who is present so no one slips through the cracks. Administration can be a kind of justice when it serves people instead of consuming them.

But counting can become reducing. And once people are reduced, it becomes easy to treat them like burdens instead of souls.

Before any institution counts you, Adonai has spoken your name. The Unseen Father does not inventory His children. In Jesus Christ, that naming became flesh. The Shepherd came close enough to be measured and registered—numbered under an empire's census—so that no one who feels reduced would stand alone.

Earth counts to administer.
Heaven counts to remember.

On Sunday a parish can tally heads for fire code, then turn and do something utterly different: the priest lifts the Host and says, "The Body of Christ," and your "Amen" is not a checkbox. It is consent to be claimed as a person. Later, in the hush of confession, you are not processed. You are listened to. Sin named without you being shamed into a category. Absolution spoken like a door opening.

"Their names were taken, that they might be remembered and nourished by the good word of God" (Moroni 6:4).

Names for nourishment, not management.

Jubilees imagines names held "before the Lord . . . continually" (Jubilees 6:13).

Enoch sees "the books of the living" opened (1 Enoch 47:3).

Not for humiliation—for remembrance.

Grace precedes the form. Gift comes before obligation.

MIKA AND THE ENVELOPE WITH TEETH

Mika is eleven—small enough that adults still speak over him, old enough to hear what they mean.

He lives with his mother in a flat where the hallway light flickers. The air smells of radiator heat and overboiled pasta. The kitchen table is the homework desk. Space is rationed like bread.

One Tuesday he comes home and finds his mother staring at an envelope as if it has teeth. Official logo. Thick paper. Polite language with quiet consequences.

"Is it bills?" he asks, backpack sliding off one shoulder.

"No," she says. "Paperwork."

"The kind that wants to know everything," he mutters, and surprises himself with the sharpness in his voice.

Pages slide out: boxes and check marks, blanks trying to compress a life into a summary.

How many live here.
What language.
What work.
What income.
What assistance.
What limitations.
What conditions.

Mika watches her pen hover over a question about health limitations. He sees the pause that looks like shame—the kind that tries to fold a person smaller.

He has watched her fill out housing forms, school forms, medical forms. Always the same small violence: the demand to become legible.

With a child's logic he thinks: If you tick the wrong box, your life will be punished for it.

"Just don't do it," he says.

She looks at him as if he has suggested they stop gravity. For a moment something in her face softens—almost hope.

"If I don't," she says, "there are consequences."

He hates that word. It sounds like a door closing.

She reads aloud, low: "Do you have a condition that limits your daily activities?"

Mika thinks of the stairs where her knee locks. The nights she sits very still because moving hurts. He hates the box.

And she checks it anyway—not because she wants to be reduced, but because she wants to be truthful. The form will record a category. Adonai keeps a name.

"O LORD, you have searched me and known me" (Ps 139:1). "Not one of them is forgotten in God's sight . . . even the hairs of your head are all counted" (Luke 12:6–7).

That is not surveillance. That is intimacy.

So Mika does something foolish, brave, and entirely human. He takes a pencil and writes at the top of the page—not inside a box, not in the designated spot. Just:

Mika.

His mother laughs once, startled, like a window opening.

"They didn't ask for that."

"I know," he says, cheeks warm. "But I'm here."

THE TABLE WHERE BOXES BECOME FACES AGAIN

Days later the form is still half-finished. Mika does homework while his mother stares at questions that make her feel small.

Then there is a knock—not loud, not demanding.

His mother stiffens anyway. Her body has learned that knocks mean obligation.

A woman from church stands there holding a plate covered in foil. The smell of garlic and warm bread slips into the hallway like quiet kindness.

"Hi," she says. "I'm Hannah. Is this a bad time?"

Mika's mother's reflex rises: *We're fine.* The lie forms quickly because it is practiced.

Hannah does not rush. She waits—patient, unafraid.

"It's . . . been a week," Mika's mother admits.

Hannah steps in and notices the form without making it a spectacle.

"Those can be heavy," she says. "Would it help if I sat with you while you do it?"

Pride rises, sharp and protective. Then exhaustion overtakes it.

"Yes," Mika's mother whispers.

So they sit. Hannah reads questions aloud. Mika's mother answers. They pause when it gets hard. Tea steam curls between them. A few unexpected laughs appear.

The form gets filled out, not as surrender, but as steadiness. Not management—accompaniment.

"Bear one another's burdens, and in this way you will fulfill the law of Christ" (Gal 6:2).

Burdens include food, yes. They also include staying at a table with paperwork and helping someone keep her dignity.

The Ruach often moves like this—not in spectacle, but in patient presence.

THE COUNTING THAT MATTERS MOST

The world catechizes you into a colder gospel: you matter if you are productive, tidy, easy to manage.

But Adonai does not bow to the ledger: "The LORD . . . looks on the heart" (1 Sam 16:7). And the seal is older than paperwork: "The Lord knows those who are his" (2 Tim 2:19).

Because Jesus Christ has carried our humanity into the heart of the Unseen Father, we are free to live covenant life without terror of the ledger.

Free to count in order to serve.
Free to remember instead of reduce.
Free to see instead of manage.

If the world counts to control, let covenant people count to care: to notice who has not been called, who has not been fed, who has gone quiet under forms and shame and silence.

And if you are the one drowning, hear this cleanly: you are not surplus. You have a name. The Unseen Father has not forgotten it. Jesus Christ has not mistaken you for a problem.

PRACTICE

Lend a hand. Keep it specific.

1. **Speak a name back into the world (today).** Choose one person treated like a case—neighbor, worker, lonely elder, a parent at the school gate. Use their name once in a sentence that isn't a request.
2. **Do paperwork mercy (within seven days).** Offer one concrete hour: "I can sit with you for sixty minutes on ___ to do the form/call/appointment." Bring tea. Read slowly. Stay until one step is finished.
3. **Interrupt reduction (this week).** When humans are spoken of like problems—"they're draining," "they're a burden,"

"those people"—say one clear sentence: "That's a person." Then ask, "What would help them this week?"

Zion is not built by perfect systems. Zion grows where a kettle boils, a chair is pulled out, and the counted are allowed to be known.

LESSON TEN

Cartography of the Thousand Million Thrones

MONEY IS NOT EVIL. But in a fallen world it rarely stays a simple tool. It becomes contested ground—one more place where a heart can be claimed.

This age trains you to handle money like pebbles. Digits turn abstract. Transfers become ghosts sliding from screen to screen. We say it's "just money," as if it carries no spiritual weather, as if it doesn't decide who sleeps warm and who learns to be quiet with hunger.

Money is a tool until it asks for worship.

So let the gospel sit where it belongs: first. Jesus Christ has already stepped into our poverty and fear. He was born into a world of taxes and counted bread, where widows were overlooked and the poor were easily erased. He carried false masters to the Cross, and He rose with a kingdom no market can price.

Because He has already claimed you, you are free to look money in the face and say, *You will not rule me.*

What ruins us is not spreadsheets. It's when we treat money as neutral and then let it decide what is human. Numbers begin to speak, and we obey without calling it worship.

Scripture calls it what it is: "No one can serve two masters. . . . You cannot serve God and wealth" (Matt 6:24).

That is not a budgeting tip. It is a revelation about allegiance.

THE REALM ABOVE THE REALM

Set this stone under your feet: the Unseen Father does not need your totals in order to know your name.

"The rich and the poor have this in common: the LORD is the maker of them all" (Prov 22:2).

Adonai does not confuse a balance sheet with a soul. In the gospel, no human being is an economic unit. You are a son or daughter made in God's image, and Jesus Christ proved your weight by taking flesh, taking wounds, and refusing to discard you.

Wealth does not have to make you cruel. It only has to make you distant.

And distance is how love dies.

Jubilees warns what happens when gain outgrows covenant memory. "The sons shall convict their fathers and their elders of sin" (Jubilees 23:16).

Mormon names the scandal of devotion that ignores bodies: "Why have ye polluted the holy church of God? . . . Why do ye adorn yourselves . . . and yet suffer the hungry . . . to pass by you, and notice them not?" (Mormon 8:37).

God is not impressed by scale. He is moved by mercy. The Church has said the same with sterner clarity across her catholic memory: surplus is not anonymous. The bread you clutch already has a claimant.

JONAS AND THE NUMBER THAT WALKED PAST HIM

There is a man named Jonas.

In his city, the news announces a miracle: a thousand million pledged for renewal. Politicians pose. Developers smile in hard hats. Cameras love clean helmets and fresh signage. Everyone speaks as if salvation has arrived with a ribbon-cutting.

Jonas lives three bus stops away from the cameras.

In winter, his flat breathes cold. The radiator clicks like it wants to help and cannot. The air smells of damp wool and reheated water. Heat is a memory. Meat is a rumor. He wears two coats indoors and boils water to trick his bones into believing they are safe.

He hears about the billion while stirring instant soup. He laughs once—not because it's funny, but because it doesn't touch him. The number walks past him like a lord stepping over a servant.

People can say "a billion" with a straight face while a child learns to eat slower so the bowl will last longer. Jonas doesn't speak policy language, but he knows what it feels like to be invisible.

Invisibility breeds a temptation that pretends to be wisdom: stop hoping, protect yourself, harden. It is despair wearing credentials.

Jonas counts and calculates, choosing between needs that should never compete. Some nights anger rises, then shame for the anger, as if pain were a moral failure. Bitterness offers itself as relief.

Then the turn comes, small and unphotographed. Jonas does not escape pressure by becoming strong. He begins to resist by refusing worship. Not because his heart is steady, but because Jesus Christ is faithful, and the Ruach can teach a frightened heart how to soften without being destroyed.

THE MEASURE HEAVEN USES

Scripture refuses the tyranny of totals.

"For the love of money is a root of all kinds of evil" (1 Tim 6:10)

Enoch echoes it: "Woe to you who acquire silver and gold in unrighteousness" (1 Enoch 94:8–9).

The warning contains mercy. God is not trying to take life from you. He is trying to give it back by breaking the spell of a counterfeit throne.

Jesus Christ exposed the lie without humiliating the small. He watched the impressive offerings. Then a poor widow placed two small coins in the treasury, and He named her gift greater (Mark 12:41–44). Not because poverty is holy, but because love is. God saw her fully.

Money is not neutral ground. It is contested territory. But you are not fighting alone. The Cross is where every false throne was judged in advance.

And when the Church lives from her Eucharistic center, almsgiving is not a hobby. It is the shape of communion. One Bread received—then translated outward until the poor are not managed. They are honored as kin.

You can watch it happen if you pay attention.

A basket passes down a pew. Coins clink. A father folds a bill like a secret and drops it in without looking around. An old woman's hands shake as she gives what she can. Then the altar: bread lifted, wine lifted, the Body broken, the Blood poured out—not for the deserving, but for the hungry.

And later, in a narrow confessional, you say what you did with fear. You name what you clutched. You admit the small violences: the indifference, the self-protection, the convenient forgetting. You hear words you did not earn: *I absolve you.* And you walk out into the world a little less owned.

Grace does not make you naïve. It makes you free.

THE JAR BEHIND THE COUNTER

Jonas works at a small shop that keeps the city alive—late-night bread, cheap batteries, milk that spoils too fast, small necessities people pretend not to need until they do.

Behind the counter he keeps a jar. No label. No announcement. A practice of quiet resistance.

Into it go small coins. Forgotten change. Overpayment refused. Mites shaved from a wage that barely exists.

Once a month he slips an envelope, anonymous, to an elderly neighbor whose electricity was cut last winter. His hands tremble the first time. He worries it won't be enough. He worries he'll be seen.

He does it anyway.

"And your Father who sees in secret will reward you" (Matt 6:4).

Zion is not built by spectacular gifts. Zion is built by patterns that refuse false thrones. From the outside, they look ordinary. From the inside, they feel like worship.

THE FINAL AUDIT

Money does not last. Markets roar and collapse. Illness drains accounts. Fortunes vanish in a season. There is coming a day when all of it is named truthfully—not to crush you, but to free you.

"For all of us must appear before the judgment seat of Christ" (2 Cor 5:10).

That accounting will not be conducted in totals. It will be conducted in love.

"For where your treasure is, there your heart will be also" (Matt 6:21).

Treasure in heaven is not stored currency. It is a heart reshaped toward mercy, integrity, and shared life. A heart that has learned—sometimes through tears—that Jesus Christ is a better Master than fear.

Mercy is the only currency that survives judgment.

PRACTICE

Choose what you will actually keep.

1. **Name the throne (today).** Write one word for what money promises you: security, status, control, numbness. Then pray one sentence (out loud if you can): "Jesus Christ, be Lord here." Close by handing God one specific fear: "I am afraid of ___."
2. **Start a mercy line (within seven days).** Create one small channel for giving that you can sustain: a jar, an envelope, or a budget line. Choose a fixed amount, even if it's modest. Place the first gift this week and aim it at a real person or local need.

3. **Interrupt the alibi (this week).** When need gets dismissed as "impractical," say one clear sentence: "We are choosing what to fund." Then ask, "What can we fund for mercy this week?" Finish with one act you can complete, not just plan—a grocery bag delivered, a bill helped, a meal shared, a travel fare paid.

Zion grows without fanfare. Let love rule your numbers, and your numbers will stop trying to rule your soul.

LESSON ELEVEN

Cartography of the Shadow-Writers

THE GOSPEL DOES NOT bless outcomes as holiness; it blesses conversion. In Jesus Christ—confessed with the Church in the Name of Father, Son, and Holy Spirit—we are freed from the tyranny of "winning" and invited into truth-telling communion, where hidden lives are no longer edited for survival but offered in repentance and fidelity.

It's easy to be impressed by the ones who return draped in flags. We call survival righteousness. We assume victory proves truth. Part of the attraction is relief: if the winners are blessed, we don't have to ask what their victory cost.

But the Unseen Father does not baptize expediency. Adonai does not call success holy merely because it succeeded. Jesus Christ does not kneel before the "right side of history."

Empires catechize their children with one quiet creed: blessed are the winners. Heaven teaches a different lesson, often through those whose names are rewritten by other people's victories. Jewish witness literature trembles with it: "And behold! He cometh with ten thousands of His holy ones to execute judgment upon all" (1 Enoch 1:9).

Bring it closer. You and I learn to edit ourselves to survive—what to say, what not to say, which truths are too expensive in mixed company. In small ways, we become shadow-writers.

THERE WAS ONCE A FLAG BEARER

A man named Marek grew up in a country repeatedly conquered and renamed. Borders shifted while he learned to walk; flags changed while he learned to write.

His father taught him survival: work hard, stay quiet, don't attract the attention of men who write reports. His mother taught him something quieter, spoken over thin soup: *Adonai sees. Even here.*

At eighteen, Marek entered law school believing justice and law walked together. Then a jurist said, calmly, like arithmetic, "Every revolution that triumphs is justified. Every revolution that fails is unjustified."

The room nodded. Marek did not. Not heroically—just with a stubborn nausea. That night he read, "I saw . . . in the place of justice, wickedness was there" (Eccl 3:16).

Years later, when economies cracked and streets tightened with fear, he was invited into a smaller room. Men spoke softly: You are loyal. You are clever. Your country needs you. Marek told himself he would prevent violence, protect the vulnerable, serve the greater good. No one begins by calling himself a shadow-writer.

A warning from a road I once used for discernment still cuts cleanly: "It is wisdom in God that these things should be shown unto you, that thereby ye may repent" (Ether 8:23).

At the first document, Marek's hand hovered. One breath of hesitation, then the pen moved anyway.

He crossed borders under cover. Observe. Listen. Report. Officially he was a trade representative. Truly he was an editor of other people's lives. He never fired a weapon, but he learned the language that makes damage feel clean: lesser evil, preventive work, strategic necessity. Outcomes, he told himself, justified methods.

The arrest came on a rainy evening, almost polite. A hand on his arm. Papers requested. Fluorescent buzz. Then the metallic taste of fear when he realized the game was over.

He was tried and imprisoned. Foreign newspapers called him unstable. His own government denied knowing him. Winter settled into the walls. In the cold he wondered which record would outlast him—the file calling him criminal or the report calling him an asset. He realized neither would survive the next treaty.

Governments rewrite stories faster than bullets erase names.

And slowly he began to sense a third archive, neither the state's nor the press's.

THE ARCHIVE NO ONE EDITS

Scripture is unsentimental about hidden things: "For all of us must appear before the judgment seat of Christ" (2 Cor 5:10). "Nothing secret will not become known" (Luke 12:2).

In that cell, Marek's religion of outcomes died. Success no longer shielded him. Silence stripped away his defenses until conscience spoke plainly. During upheaval, attention drifted. Marek and two others escaped—not heroically, but bleeding and afraid. He ran until his lungs burned and his thoughts turned to ash. He prayed only not to die.

Then, for the first time, he told the truth aloud: *Unseen Father, I have lived for outcomes. Have mercy on me.*

Confession did not erase his past. It opened him to repentance. Strangers fed him without questions. A farmer offered bread without speeches. Mercy arrived without ideology, and something in him shifted. He began to see people as souls instead of pieces on a board.

When he finally returned home, his family wept as if receiving someone resurrected. But peace did not settle. He had lived too long in shadows to pretend the light was easy.

Still craving vindication, he went back to the capital. He wanted his name cleared without his heart fully changed. What followed was theater. They charged him with manageable offenses, then defended him publicly as a loyal son of the homeland. From traitor to patriot in one act—not because he became holy, but because the outcome changed.

Here is the heresy you already recognize:

- If betrayal succeeds, it becomes loyalty.

- If violence succeeds, it becomes security.
- Failure alone is unforgivable.

Success is not a sacrament.

Jesus Christ never said, "Blessed are the winners." He said, "Blessed are the peacemakers" (Matt 5:9).

Even Gideon had to learn that Adonai refuses to let victory become an idol: "The troops with you are too many . . . Israel would only take the credit" (Judg 7:2).

At the center stands Christ Himself. He did not manipulate outcomes in secret rooms. He walked openly. He healed publicly. He refused to edit Himself to satisfy power. By worldly arithmetic, He "failed," humiliated and crucified. The Unseen Father answered the world's verdict with resurrection: "The stone that the builders rejected has become the chief cornerstone" (Ps 118:22).

That should frighten us—unless grace goes first. Here is the grace: Jesus Christ has already entered the fire we fear, carrying hidden sin and public shame. Because He has gone first, we are free to stop living as editors and begin living as disciples.

Years after his release, Marek stepped into a small church while flags changed outside yet again. The air smelled faintly of candle wax and wet wool. He waited in a line that moved slowly toward a narrow wooden box. When his turn came, he knelt. The screen hid the priest's face. Marek's hands trembled anyway.

"Bless me, Father. . ."

Truth came out without decoration. Names. Scenes. The careful lies. The sentences he had written that rearranged other people's lives.

Then, quietly: *Ego te absolvo.* The words did not flatter him. They cut him loose.

At the altar, the liturgy did what it always does—plain, bodily, unembarrassed. A Host lifted. A chalice raised. A people breathing together, confessing together, receiving together.

"The Body of Christ."

"Amen."

Repentance was not a mood. It was a surrender with a voice and a body. Sin named. Mercy received. A new pattern learned in communion, with counsel and accountability that keeps the light from becoming performance.

The Church does not exist to protect outcomes. She exists to form saints—people who can tell the truth without bargaining.

WHEN THE RUACH BEGINS TO SPEAK

Years later, the reading was simple and merciless:

"Nothing is covered up that will not be uncovered" (Luke 12:2).

The Ruach did not only accuse him. He invited him.

Marek understood that history was not the final author of his life. Spy, traitor, hero—none of those names would endure. Beneath every story was a plainer sentence: *What you do in the dark is what you are becoming.*

No one is saved by standing on the right side of history. History itself will be judged. The final measure is not outcome but conversion, and that is mercy. A man rewritten by governments can still be rewritten by Christ. You can stop living as a shadow-writer and live as someone whose truth is not for sale.

This is also how Zion learns peace: not by propaganda, not by edited narratives, but by truth-telling communion—justice without hatred, mercy without denial. A people practicing fidelity when expediency would "work" better.

PRACTICE

Choose one act of light that costs you something.

1. **Tell one truth you usually edit (today).** Name the place where you curate yourself to "win." Speak one clean sentence there: an apology, a confession, a firm *no*, or a gentle *that isn't true.* No speech to protect your image.

2. **Refuse one success story you use as cover (within seven days).** Write the narrative you lean on: *It worked, so it must be right.* Name what it excused. Then pray one line: *Jesus Christ, reorder my allegiance.* If repair is possible, take one step toward it this week.
3. **Choose one mercy that looks like losing (this week).** Do one act that costs status or comfort: forgive first, protect someone smaller, tell the truth when silence would advance you. Make it concrete. Finish it.

The Ruach does not merely expose the shadows. He trains the body for daylight.

LESSON TWELVE

Cartography of All Things Seen and Unseen

History isn't a classroom. It's a furnace. It doesn't only tell us what happened—it reveals what we become when heat arrives.

In Jesus Christ—confessed with the Church in the Name of the Father, and of the Son, and of the Holy Spirit—there is a refusal built into our bones. Not panic. Not propaganda. Not numbness. A sacramental obedience that keeps the heart human and turns outward toward the neighbor.

It's tempting to treat history like a tidy diagram: arrows, villains, moral certainty drawn from a safe seat. I do it too. Then the world grows old again—dry timber that can build and still burn.

The Unseen Father does not need headlines to know when a civilization is cracking. Adonai hears the panic behind speeches, the hunger behind policies, the exhaustion behind slogans. Christ is not far off. He entered our history in flesh—close enough to touch lepers, to carry wood, to be misunderstood.

"What has been is what will be . . . there is nothing new under the sun" (Eccl 1:9).

Begin with a human being, because theology without flesh becomes smoke.

ELIAS AND THE WAR THAT ARRIVED IN SMALLER PORTIONS

Elias is a clerk in a port city where the air tastes of coal and salt. He keeps ledgers for cargo he will never own—wheat, steel, oil—things that become "progress" in speeches and survival in kitchens. He lives in a narrow flat with a stubborn stove.

His wife, Marta, slices meat thinner than dignity should require. Quietly, as if quiet could soften scarcity. Their son, Joachim, watches and pretends not to watch. Elias sees the boy's eyes linger, then look away—hunger made invisible by shame.

Uniforms multiply. Measuring uniforms. Inspecting uniforms. Horizon-watching uniforms. In taverns, men talk about honor and destiny, as if war were weather: it has to happen.

Elias keeps quiet. He knows a law of surviving anxious powers: if you want to live, do not become interesting.

A boy runs past, waving a newspaper map—arrows, coastlines, imagined landings, imagined victories. Elias feels cold behind his ribs. He understands the map's purpose is not prediction but permission. Maps teach permission. When a people calls violence "inevitable," conscience learns to excuse itself. Fear gets renamed wisdom. Appetite becomes king.

"Those conflicts and disputes among you, where do they come from? Do they not come from your cravings that are at war within you?" (Jas 4:1).

That night Elias comes home. Joachim is asleep over his schoolbook, ink smudged on his thumb. Marta mends a shirt by lamplight, the needle moving like prayer. Elias heats water, breaks yesterday's bread, and slides the larger piece toward his son. He hesitates for one heartbeat—tomorrow—and then does it anyway.

The Ruach trains some people like this: not with spectacle, but with hands.

THE LETTER THAT TAUGHT THE CHILD TO FLINCH

Weeks pass. The harbor grows busy, then quiet in a rehearsed way. Cargo disappears into "official channels." Then a letter arrives—not to Elias, but to the building: preparedness, storage, behavior.

Marta reads it twice and folds it like someone handling a blade.

Joachim asks if it's practice.

Elias wants to wrap the boy in soft words. He also knows false peace poisons as surely as fear. So he answers gently, without pretending.

"It's practice for something people are acting like they can't see."

That night Elias watches his son sleep, face unarmored, and prays with his stomach tight: protect him, yes—but keep him from learning to worship violence. Do not let fear become his religion. Christ has carried prayers like this into the dark.

SEEN AND UNSEEN

Elias stands by the docks. Black water, black sky, ships like withheld breath. You can see uniforms, ships, ration cards, slogans. You cannot photograph the moment a conscience steps back from mercy. You cannot map the inner drift from *this is wrong* to *this must be done.*

And yet that unseen drift is the battleground, because Adonai's accounting is not only about outcomes. It is about what we became while we chased them.

Jewish witness texts say it without anesthesia—"every sin is every day recorded in heaven" (1 Enoch 98:8). "Calamity follows on calamity . . . and tribulation on tribulation" (Jubilees 23:13).

Elias whispers into the dark: You see this.

The answer does not thunder. It steadies. Tyranny is not ultimate. The God who is unseen is not absent.

"He who sits in the heavens laughs; the Lord has them in derision" (Ps 2:4).

Not because suffering is funny, but because empires are not final. The Resurrection is God's refusal to let death write the ending.

THE TWO FALSE GOSPELS

When fear spreads, two counterfeit gospels appear.

Panic-obedience: do whatever sounds urgent, surrender conscience to the crowd, call cruelty "necessary," call hard-heartedness "maturity."

Clever distance: mock everything so you never have to be responsible, call despair "realism," keep your heart cold and your hands "clean."

Both end the same way: a soul that has stopped loving.

I keep one line as a corrective because it names restraint in an age that praises blood: a people who "did not delight in bloodshed . . . but . . . delighted in . . . peace" (Alma 48:11).

The gospel offers a third way: not spectacle and not numbness, but covenant life born from grace—slow, embodied, merciful, untheatrical. Because Christ has entered our fear, we are free to practice a different kind of obedience: shepherd-shaped living.

WHERE ZION BEGINS

Elias cannot control the harbor or the headlines. He controls one thing: what kind of man he will become.

On Sunday he goes to the parish with a tightened throat. The nave smells of wax and wet wool. He kneels. The Kyrie rises and falls like breath. At the altar the priest lifts bread that looks too small to matter, and the bell rings—thin, insistent—like heaven tapping the world on the shoulder.

Elias opens his mouth and receives. Not an idea. A Body. Christ presses Himself into a frightened people and does not flinch.

After Mass he stands in line for confession because he can feel what this age is trying to carve into him. Behind the screen he whispers what he has become in miniature: contempt, hoarding, the little rehearsals of hardness. The priest's voice is plain, almost tired, and it lands like water: *I absolve you.* Mercy does not decorate life. Mercy rebuilds it.

People talk about storing food. Prudence is not betrayal. But the real test waits in the hallway: an elderly neighbor with no coal, a family with a fevered child, rent that won't meet the month.

The community begins to move, not as a mob but as a body.

"I have extra."
"I can drive."
"Let's not let them be alone."

This is sacramental imagination in plain clothes. Grace refusing to stay abstract. Bread. Coal. A knock on a door. The Church being what she is meant to be—communion, not commentary.

Elias goes home and sets one extra place at the table, once, as a decision: we will not become a closed house. The next day he knocks on Mr. Novak's door and asks what he needs. Pride hesitates. Loneliness answers: "Coal." Elias brings coal, not as a savior but as a neighbor.

Joachim watches. The child is being catechized—not into militarism or cynicism, but into discipleship. Elias does not become merciful to earn God. He becomes merciful because mercy has found him first.

Mercy keeps the world human.

THE UNSEEN AUDIT

When war is called necessary, ask—quietly, without theater—who profits. When peace is mocked as weakness, notice who sharpens knives. When mapmakers fantasize about blood, understand consciences are being trained.

You do not have to carry history to resist that training. You only have to refuse, today, to let your heart be remodeled into something inhuman.

PRACTICE

Refuse the training. Choose the neighbor.

1. **Make one mercy-move (today).** Do one concrete act that costs something small: share food, check on a neighbor, offer a ride, bring coal or bread, stay ten extra minutes with someone who is afraid.
2. **Interrupt one "necessary cruelty" (this week).** When someone says, "It has to be done," ask one clean question: "Who benefits?" Then add: "Who pays—and what would mercy require of us this week?"
3. **Practice obedience without fear (for seven days).** Each day ask the Ruach, "Where am I hardening?" Then do one softening act with a finish line: apologize, forgive, reconcile, tell the truth, refuse contempt in one conversation.

Keep your heart human. Let it cost you.

CODA

Cartography of the Walker

You have read twelve maps.

But maps are not the point.
Feet are.

A map folded neatly in your pocket cannot change the soil. Only a walker can—baptized flesh, a life received and offered again, in Jesus Christ, confessed with the Church in the Name of the Father, and of the Son, and of the Holy Spirit.

Long ago Adonai said to Abram, "Walk before me, and be blameless" (Gen 17:1). And Isaiah gave the quiet instruction: "This is the way; walk in it" (Isa 30:21). The command has always been simple. It has always required a body.

Jesus Christ did not come to hand you a system. He came to take the road Himself—dust on His feet, mercy in His hands—walking toward the wounded and the corrupt, toward the ashamed, toward Jerusalem, knowing what waited there.

And He did not leave you as a solitary pilgrim.

He gathers a people—His body—and teaches that our steps are not private victories but communal fidelity. "Walk in love, as Christ loved us and gave himself up for us" (Eph 5:2).

"If we live by the Spirit, let us also be guided by the Spirit" (Gal 5:25). The Ruach keeps pace—through Scripture, through the Church's memory, through ordinary disciplines that keep us honest: confession without theater, obedience without servility, courage without domination.

Kneel. Say the plain truth. Hear the words you do not deserve and cannot purchase: *I absolve you.* Then stand and return to your life without applause.

The Cross was not efficient. Grace came first.

"There is therefore now no condemnation for those who are in Christ Jesus" (Rom 8:1). Shame is not your homeland. The Unseen Father is—His house, His mercy, His adoption of you in Christ.

You are not sent to build Zion by force.
You are not sent to repair the world with arguments.
You are not sent to perform holiness until it becomes convincing.

You are sent to walk as one who belongs: grounded, accountable, Eucharistically fed, learning communion rather than spectacle.

So enter rooms without armor.
Carry responsibility without domination.
Meet conflict without cruelty.

Receive rest without apology, for "a Sabbath rest still remains for the people of God" (Heb 4:9). Even older Jewish witness remembers Sabbath as a holy interruption set into creation—an antidote to the world's frenzy, a retraining of time (Jubilees speaks this way as an older lamp along the road).

Practice repentance without display: "If we confess our sins, he who is faithful and just will forgive us and cleanse us from all unrighteousness" (1 John 1:9). Choose mercy when no one sees: "Be merciful, just as your Father is merciful" (Luke 6:36). God has always desired mercy more than sacrifice (Matt 9:13).

There is another map you know. It urges speed, worships image, rewards suspicion, keeps score. That map is loud.

The kingdom of God is quieter. It grows the way a path forms across a field—not by proclamation, but by persistence.

One step.
Then another.

Zion is not a skyline. It is a trail worn into the earth by ordinary obedience—communion chosen when nobody applauds, forgiveness chosen when hardness would have earned admiration.

Ancient witnesses echo this, too, as lamps rather than law: Enoch urging love of righteousness, walking in paths of peace; holiness as a people formed over time. A path repeated becomes a people formed.

So choose one small mile.
Not a revolution. A mile.

And within Restoration witness—received as testimony and longing—one voice pleads with stark simplicity: "And now, my beloved brethren, I would that ye should come unto Christ, who is the Holy One of Israel, and partake of his salvation, and the power of his redemption. Yea, come unto him, and offer your whole souls as an offering unto him, and continue in fasting and praying, and endure to the end; and as the Lord liveth ye will be saved" (Omni 1:26).

A phone call made.
A bitterness released.
A table opened.
A boundary held without contempt.
A confession spoken plainly.
A rest received as obedience.

Let your shoes carry mercy where slogans cannot.

When you fail—and you will—do not kneel before shame as if it were your king. "As you therefore have received Christ Jesus the Lord, continue to live your lives in him" (Col 2:6). A stumble does not erase the road.

The Ruach will steady you. Christ will not lose you. In the communion of saints, you will learn what you could not learn alone: fidelity is often just staying on the path.

One day, without fanfare, you may look behind you and see that others have begun to follow the quiet line your faithfulness pressed into the dust.

That is the cartography of the walker: a road made visible by love.

Walk before Adonai.
Leave tracks the weary can trust.

APPENDIX

Guardrails & Crisis Support

GUARDRAILS

THESE ARE NOT TECHNIQUES for controlling God. They are covenantal guardrails—habits that protect mercy-bearing people in a world that often mistakes endurance for performance. They keep me near Jesus Christ, near Scripture, and near the church.

1. **Scripture first.** Every impression bows to the word already given. If there is tension, Scripture wins.
2. **Community counsel.** I test experiences with pastors, elders, and trauma-wise mentors. Solitary certainty is unsafe; I invite correction.
3. **Fruit.** If something yields love, repentance, holiness, humility, and service, I keep it. If it breeds pride, fear, secrecy, or harm, I release it.
4. **Time.** Truth strengthens when waited on; falsehood demands urgency. I do not rush major decisions.
5. **Sobriety.** Grace does not fear psychology. I examine trauma patterns and triggers honestly, and seek clinical support when needed.
6. **Ordinary obedience.** Genuine spiritual experiences send me back to prayer, sacrament, fellowship, work, and service—not away from them.

7. **No new doctrine.** Jesus Christ is the final Word. Nothing I see, feel, or imagine adds to Him.
8. **Peace over pressure.** The Spirit convicts without coercion. If an "impression" demands secrecy, shames others, isolates me, or bypasses conscience, I set it aside.
9. **Boundaries.** Any "word" that asks for money, isolation, secrecy, or special access is rejected and reported.

These guardrails exist because covenant is meant to form love—not spectacle, not control, not hidden harm.

CRISIS & MENTAL HEALTH SUPPORT

If you are carrying wounds from abuse, violence, coercion, or despair:

- **Immediate danger:** Call your local emergency number (e.g., 999 / 911 / 112).
- **Need to speak to someone now:** Contact a trusted crisis helpline in your country.
- **Clerical or spiritual abuse:** Reach out to independent survivor-advocacy groups and safeguarding offices not connected to the alleged abuser.
- **Document and report:** Preserve messages or evidence; seek legal or medical care as appropriate; do not confront an abuser alone.
- **For church leaders:** Believe disclosures. Do not promise secrecy. Follow local law. Remove accused persons from ministry during investigation. Protect children and the vulnerable above reputation.

Note: Helpline numbers can change over time. If a number below is inactive, visit a verified directory such as *befrienders.org* or *findahelpline.com* to locate current support in your area.

DIRECTORIES

- befrienders.org
- findahelpline.com

UNITED STATES

- **988 Suicide and Crisis Lifeline:** Call or text 988; chat at 988lifeline.org.
- **RAINN National Sexual Assault Hotline:** 800–656-HOPE (4673).
- **National Domestic Violence Hotline:** 800–799-SAFE (7233); text START to 88788.

CANADA

- **9-8-8 Suicide Crisis Helpline:** Call or text 988.
- **Kids Help Phone:** 800–668-6868; text 686868.

UNITED KINGDOM

- **Samaritans:** 116 123 (24/7 free emotional support).
- **Refuge:** 0808 2000 247 (national domestic abuse helpline).
- **Rape Crisis England and Wales:** 0808 500 2222.

EUROPEAN UNION / EEA

- **Emergency:** 112.
- **Emotional Support Helpline:** 116 123 (where active).
- **Victims of Crime Helpline:** 116 006 (where active).
- **Child Helpline:** 116 111 (where active).

AUSTRALIA

- **Lifeline:** 13 11 14.
- **1800RESPECT:** 1800 737 732.

NEW ZEALAND

- **1737—Need to Talk?:** Call or text 1737.
- **Safe to Talk:** 0800 044 334; text 4334.
- **Women's Refuge:** 0800 733 843.
- **Shine:** 0508 744 633.

INDIA

- **Emergency:** 112.
- **KIRAN:** 1800–599-0019.
- **Tele MANAS:** 14416.
- **CHILDLINE:** 1098.
- **Women's Helpline:** 181.
- **iCALL (TISS Counseling):** 9152987821 / 022–25521111.

AFRICA

- **SADAG Suicide Crisis Line (South Africa):** 0800 567 567.

ASIA (OUTSIDE INDIA)

For country-specific support numbers, use:

- befrienders.org
- findahelpline.com

www.ingramcontent.com/pod-product-compliance
Lightning Source LLC
LaVergne TN
LVHW020649100826
845148LV00012B/2395

* 9 7 9 8 3 8 5 2 8 0 6 5 0 *